THE
MIND of LIGHT

THE SUPRAMENTAL MANIFESTATION
UPON EARTH

Sri Aurobindo

**INTRODUCTION AND ANNOTATED BIBLIOGRAPHY
BY ROBERT A. MCDERMOTT**

**LOTUS
PRESS**

Twin Lakes, WI
U.S.A.

First Published in 1971

Second Enlarged U.S. Edition 2003
Published by Lotus Press by arrangement with Sri Aurobindo Ashram, Copyright Department, Pondicherry, India 605002.

Lotus Press, P.O. Box 325, Twin Lakes, Wisconsin 53181.
Web: www.lotuspress.com   Email: lotuspress@lotuspress.com
(800) 824-6396

Ghose, Sri Aurobindo, 1872-1950
The Mind of Light

ISBN: 0-940985-70-5

Library of Congress Control Number: 2003111977

Printed in the United States of America.

CONTENTS

INTRODUCTION

THE FORMATION
OF SRI AUROBINDO'S VISION

Among the many sayings of Sri Aurobindo and the Mother, which are posted throughout the Sri Aurobindo Ashram in Pondicherry, South India, the following is typical: "The world is preparing for a big change. Will you help?" According to Sri Aurobindo's vision, this change refers to the advance of human and cosmic evolution. Sri Aurobindo's personal life and philosophy of Integral Yoga attest to the fact that this transformation can only come about by man's cooperation with the Supermind.[1]

Forty years before writing *The Mind of Light*, Sri Aurobindo's commitment to the transformation or liberation of India included plans for armed insurrection against the British government of India, a program of mass propaganda for the idea of *Swaraj* (independence), and a program of economic boycott and passive resistance.[2] Just as Sri Aurobindo in later years addressed himself to the practical, urgent crises of modern civilization, he had earlier viewed India's political struggle as part of the spiritual transformation of man. While leader of the extremist faction of the Nationalist movement, and editor of the revolutionary weekly, *Bande Mataram*, Sri Aurobindo maintained that "the true aim of the Nationalist movement is to restore the spiritual greatness of the nation by the essential preliminary of its political regeneration."[3] And again: "The movement of which the first outbreak was political, will end in a spiritual consummation."[4] Four decades later, on the celebration of Indian Independence, August 15, 1947, Sri Aurobindo again linked these dual ideals:

> For I have always held and said that India was arising, not to serve her own material interests only, to achieve

expansion, greatness, power, and prosperity-though these too she must not neglect-and certainly not like others to acquire domination of other peoples, but to live also for God and the world as a helper and leader of the whole human race. Those aims and ideals were in their natural order these: a revolution that would achieve India's freedom and her unity; the resurgence and liberation of Asia and her return to the great role which she had played in the progress of human civilization; the rise of a new, a greater, brighter, and nobler life for mankind which for its entire realization would rest outwardly on an international unification of the separate existence of the peoples, preserving and securing their national life but drawing them together into an overriding and consummating oneness; the gift by India of her spiritual knowledge and her means for the spiritualization of life to the whole race; finally, a new step in the evolution which, by uplifting the consciousness to a higher level, would begin the solution of the many problems of existence that have perplexed and vexed humanity, since men began to think and to dream of individual perfection and a perfect society.[5]

In short, the dual ideals of a total resurgence of India and the total transformation of man characterized the mature work of Aurobindo Ghose, the political revolutionary of Bengal (1905-10), and of Sri Aurobindo, the mystical Yogi of Pondicherry (1910-50). This complementarity of politics and spirituality typifies Sri Aurobindo's ability to draw diverse strains into a rich and dynamic synthesis: as he combined politics and Yoga, he also combined Western and Indian values. The conditions for this synthesizing ability were created by the highly diverse strains in his personal life.

Aurobindo Ghose was born in Calcutta on August 15, 1872, third son of a successful Bengali doctor and his wife who in her later years suffered from hysteria. When Aurobindo was five years old, he and his two older brothers were sent to the Loretto Convent School at Darjeeling. Two years later, in 1879, Aurobindo and his two brothers were sent to England, where he remained until 1893, when he was twenty years old. Despite the handicap of an inadequate financial allowance, he excelled in his studies, primarily classics, both at St. Paul's School, London, and at King's College, Cambridge. He also participated in two so-called secret societies, "Lotus and Dagger" and "Majlis," both of which were organized by students romantically dedicated to Indian independence.[6]

Although Sri Aurobindo's entire formation from the age of seven to twenty was thoroughly British (as was his father's wish), a deep longing for Indian culture must have developed in him, for he enjoyed a remarkable religious experience when he arrived at the Bombay Gate in 1893.[7] This longing for a direct experience of India led Sri Aurobindo to spend the next thirteen years at Baroda studying the Indian intellectual tradition, including several Indian languages, while serving as Professor of English and subsequently, as Vice-Principal of Baroda College. It was during this time that Sri Aurobindo wrote voluminous poetry, translated Sanskrit texts, and generally sunk his roots deep into the Indian cultural soil.

These years in Baroda served as the intellectual and spiritual base for Sri Aurobindo's five years of revolutionary activity in Calcutta, and his enormously productive years at Pondicherry from 1914-21. Sri Aurobindo himself offers an account of his spiritual growth during these years:

I began my Yoga in 1904 without a guru; in 1908 I received important help from a Mahratta Yogi and discovered the foundations of my sadhana; but from that time till the Mother came to India I received no spiritual help from anyone else. My sadhana before and afterwards was not founded upon books but upon personal experiences that crowded on me from within. But in the jail I had the Gita and the Upanishads with me, practiced the Yoga of the Gita and meditated with the help of the Upanishads, these were the only books from which I found guidance; the Veda, which I first began to read long afterwards in Pondicherry, rather confirmed what experiences I already had than was any guide to my sadhana. I sometimes turned to the Gita for light when there was a question or a difficulty and usually received help or an answer from it. It is a fact that I was hearing constantly the voice of Vivekananda speaking to me for a fortnight in the jail in my solitary meditation and felt his presence. The voice spoke only on a special and limited but very important field of spiritual experience and it ceased as soon as it had finished saying all that it had to say on that subject.[8]

As this passage indicates, Sri Aurobindo's spiritual life or sadhana (spiritual or yogic practice) was based on four religious experiences, two of which occurred prior to this withdrawal from politics in 1910.

> The first he had gained while meditating with the Maharashtrian Yogi, Vishnu Bhaskar Lele, at Baroda in January, 1908; it was the realization of the silent, spaceless and timeless Brahman gained after a complete and abiding stillness of the whole consciousness and attended at first by the overwhelming feeling and perception of the total unreality of the world, though this feeling disappeared after his second realization, which was that of the cosmic consciousness and of the Divine as all beings and all that is, which happened in the Alipore Jail. To the other two realizations, that of the supreme Reality with the static and dynamic Brahman as its two aspects and that of the higher planes of consciousness leading up to the Supermind, he was already on his way in his meditations in Alipore Jail.[9]

Of the four, the experience in the Alipore Jail is perhaps the most significant for our understanding of Sri Aurobindo's life and thought. While in solitary confinement (and during several months when he mingled with other prisoners), Sri Aurobindo meditated on the Bhagavadgita and envisioned the Supreme Lord (Vasudeva) transforming the entire human and cosmic process. As he explained in his celebrated Uttarpara Speech of 1909, God led him to accept as his own the tasks of leading India to independence, and of realizing the eternal truths of Hindu dharma.[10]

Thus, Sri Aurobindo's withdrawal from politics was not a withdrawal from the Indian or the world situation. Consistent with the ideal of karmayoga (selfless action), which he derived from the Bhagavadgita and reformulated during his years of politics and Yoga in Bengal, Sri Aurobindo "kept a close watch on all that was happening in the world and in India and actively intervened whenever necessary, but solely with a spiritual force and silent spiritual action ... It was this force which, as soon as he had attained to it, he used, at first only in a limited field of personal work, but afterward in a constant action upon the world forces."[11] His life at Pondicherry, then, was spent in seclusion precisely in order to continue working for Indian and universal liberation.

The key elements in this effort can now be delineated.

SRI AUROBINDO'S TEACHING

The last six chapters of *The Life Divine* are the fullest expression of Sri Aurobindo's vision of spiritual evolution; the opening passage of the first of these six chapters, "Man and Evolution," establishes the framework for the entire vision:

> A spiritual evolution, an evolution of consciousness in Matter in a constant developing self-formation till the form can reveal the indwelling spirit, is then the keynote, the central significant motive of the terrestrial existence. This significance is concealed at the outset by the involution of the Spirit, the Divine Reality, in a dense material Inconscience; a veil of Inconscience, a veil of insensibility of Matter hides the universal Consciousness-Force that works within it, so that the Energy, which is the first form the Force of creation assumes in the physical universe, appears to be itself inconscient and yet does the works of a vast occult Intelligence. The obscure mysterious creatrix ends indeed by delivering the secret consciousness out of its thick and tenebrous prison; but she delivers it slowly, little by little, in minute infinitesimal drops, in thin jets, in small vibrant concretions of energy and substance, of life, of mind, as if that were all she could get out through the crass obstacle, the dull reluctant medium of an inconscient stuff of existence. At first she houses herself in forms of Matter which appear to be altogether unconscious, then struggles toward mentality in the guise of living Matter and attains to it imperfectly in the conscious animal. This consciousness is at first rudimentary, mostly a half-subconscious or just conscious instinct; it develops slowly till in more organized forms of living Matter it reaches its climax of intelligence and exceeds itself in Man, the thinking animal who develops into the reasoning mental being but carries along with him even at his highest elevation the mold of original animality, the dead weight of subconscience of body, the downward pull of gravitation toward the original Inertia and Nescience, the control of an inconscient material

Nature over his conscious evolution, its power for limitation, its law of difficult development, its immense force for retardation and frustration. This control by the original Inconscience over the consciousness emerging from it takes the general shape of a mentality struggling toward knowledge but itself, in what seems to be its fundamental nature, an Ignorance. Thus hampered and burdened, mental man has still to evolve out of himself the fully conscious being, a divine manhood or a spiritual and supramental supermanhood which shall be the next product of the evolution. That transition will mark the passage from the evolution in the Ignorance to a greater evolution in the Knowledge, founded and proceeding in the light of the Superconscient and no longer in the darkness of the Ignorance and Inconscience.[12]

The process and goal described in this lengthy passage is a unified vision of human and cosmic evolution proceeding toward supramental existence by the increasing spiritualization of consciousness. As Sri Nolini Kanta Gupta notes in his excellent summary:

Sri Aurobindo's message is very simple, almost self-evident. The sum and substance of all he says is that man is growing and has to grow in consciousness till he reaches the complete and perfect consciousness, not only in his individual but in his collective, that is to say, social life. In fact, the growth of consciousness is the supreme secret of life, the master key to earthly existence.[13]

According to Sri Aurobindo's vision, as developed in *The Life Divine*, there are several levels between nature and supernature or mind and Supermind.

These gradations may be summarily described as a series of sublimations of the consciousness through Higher Mind, Illumined Mind, and Intuition, into Overmind and beyond it; there is a succession of self-transmutations at the summit of which lies the Supermind or Divine Gnosis.[14]

These gradations, furthermore, include the three levels of the lower trilogy or levels of evolution up to the present stage, mind: the mental level evolved from the vital, and the vital from the material. One of the characteristics of the entire evolutionary process is that "at each crossover, there is not only a rise in consciousness but also a reversal of consciousness, that is to say, the level attained turns back upon the preceding levels, influencing and molding them as far as possible in its own mode and law of existence."[15] Thus, the mental has transformed the material and the vital, and the supramental, through the mediation of Overmind, is beginning to transform the mental. The gradations between mental and supramental are in the process of transformation just as the material and vital stages have been taken up by consciousness into its own evolution. Evolution, then, consists in two processes, both controlled by consciousness: the outward, physical or cosmic evolution from matter to mind, and the higher, more essential and spiritual evolution from mind to Supermind.

Although the stages of cosmic evolution are philosophically rather well established,[16] the higher evolutionary stages need far more justification. Sri Aurobindo acknowledges that any account of these higher stages of consciousness "must perforce be inadequate; only certain abstract generalizations can be hazarded which may serve for an initial light of guidance."[17] He forthrightly admits that his theory of evolution is subject to doubt on the level of intelligence. From a philosophical perspective, his account of this version is far from certain. He cautions that:

> This account of the process and meaning of the terrestrial creation is at every point exposed to challenge in the mind of man himself, because the evolution is still halfway on its journey, is still in the Ignorance, is still seeking in the mind of a half-evolved humanity for its own purpose and significance. It is possible to challenge the theory of evolution on the ground that it is insufficiently founded and that it is superfluous as an explanation of the process of terrestrial existence. It is open to doubt, even if evolution is granted, whether man has the capacity to develop into a higher evolutionary being. It is also open to doubt whether the evolution is likely to go any farther than it has gone already or whether a supramental evolution, the appearance of a consummated Truth-Consciousness, a being of Knowledge, is at all probable

in the fundamental Ignorance of the earthly Nature.[18]

In contrast to this lack of certitude on the level of philosophical inquiry, Sri Aurobindo's own spiritual experience and vision confidently proclaim the inevitability of man's spiritual evolution. Indeed, since his entire philosophy issues from a yogic experience, which is both personal and transcendent, his account of spiritual evolution is but a pointer to the experiences that are the source and ultimately the corroboration of that theory. Thus, Sri Aurobindo's philosophy of Integral Yoga is a vision of personal and cosmic evolution as well as a method for its realization. Whereas his theory of evolution and integralism begs comparison with many Western philosophies, the essential function of Yoga in this theory is distinctively Indian. This blending of vision and practice, or speculation and discipline, characterizes Sri Aurobindo's penchant for Western-Indian syntheses. Further, the method of Yoga operative in this synthesis is itself a synthesis of several schools of Indian Yoga.[19] The components of both syntheses are important and instructive for an understanding of Sri Aurobindo's overall philosophy.

As he explains in his masterful work, *The Synthesis of Yoga*, Integral Yoga incorporates within itself and yet transcends the ultimate goals as well as the essential principles of the great Yogas of the Indian philosophical and religious tradition.

> On the whole, for an Integral Yoga the special methods of Rajayoga and Hathayoga may be useful at times in certain stages of the process, but are not indispensable. It is true that their principal aims must be included in the integrality of the Yoga; but they can be brought about by other means. For the methods of the Integral Yoga must be mainly spiritual, and dependence on physical methods or fixed psychic or psychophysical processes on a large scale would be the substitution of a lower for a higher action.[20]

Sri Aurobindo's Yoga is integral in that it includes the path of knowledge, or *jñana-yoga*, which "aims at the realization of the unique and supreme Self ... by the method of intellectual reflection, *vicara*, to right discrimination, *viveka*"[21]; the path of devotion or *bhakti-yoga*, which "aims at the enjoyment of the Supreme Lord and Bliss and normally utilizes the conception of the supreme Lord in His personality as the divine Lover and enjoyer of the universe"[22]; and the path of works, which "aims at the dedication of every human activity to the supreme Will."[23] Sri Aurobindo's Integral Yoga attempts to synthesize these three yogic disciplines by "some central principle common to all, which will include and utilize in the right place and proportion their particular principles."[24]

The principle that includes and transforms all three yogas is a fourth Yoga, the Yoga of self-perfection. Thus, the triple way of knowledge, will, and *Ananda* is integrated by the Yoga of spiritual and gnostic self-perfection.[25] The Yoga of self-perfection, which is the subject of the entire fourth part of *The Synthesis of Yoga*, is well summarized in the following passage:

> The object of our synthetic Yoga must ... be more integral and comprehensive, embrace all these elements or these tendencies of a larger impulse of self-perfection and harmonize them or rather unify, and in order to do that successfully it must seize on a truth that is wider than the ordinary religious and higher than the mundane principle. All life is a secret Yoga, an obscure growth of Nature toward the discovery and fulfillment of the divine principle hidden in her, which becomes progressively less obscure, more self-conscient and luminous, more self-possessed in the human being by the opening of all his instruments of knowledge, will, action, life to the Spirit within him and in the world. Mind, life, body, all the forms of our nature are the means of this growth, but they find their last perfection only by opening out to something beyond them, first, because they are not the whole of what man is, secondly, because that other something which he is, is the key of his completeness and brings a light that discovers to him the whole high and large reality of his being.[26]

Both because it integrates the Yogas of knowledge, will, and devotion, and because it opens man to the largest and most total transformation, the Yoga of self-perfection involves the "transformation of the lower and its elevation to the higher Nature."[27] This theory of transformation includes both Tantric and Vedantic elements. It is Tantric in that it takes

Energy or Shakti "as the sole effective force for all attainment."[28] It is Vedantic in its conception of energy as Maya or Nescience projecting the unreal cosmic manifold on the locus of the nondual Brahman. Thus, Sri Aurobindo sees a double motion wherein Energy seeks to establish the Divine on earth, and the Divine expresses itself through individuals and through nature.

The key to Sri Aurobindo's integral vision, then, is the transformation of the lower by the higher reaches of consciousness. According to Sri Aurobindo's vision, this transformation, which is the cooperative work of man and the Supermind, is "as great as and greater than the change which we suppose evolutionary Nature to have made in its transition from the vital animal to the fully mentalized human consciousness."[29] This great change celebrated by Sri Aurobindo and his followers is at once a visionary and a practical message: man can achieve a higher level of life by increased nonattachment, concentration, and liberation.[30] Further, this achievement is the ultimate goal and value of human and cosmic existence. Sri Aurobindo explains this fact, and summarizes his vision in the following passage.

> The divinizing of the normal material life of man and of his great secular attempt of mental and moral self-culture in the individual and the race by this integralization of a widely perfect spiritual existence would thus be the crown alike of our individual and of our common effort. Such a consummation being no other than the kingdom of heaven within reproduced in the kingdom of heaven without, would be also the true fulfillment of the great dream cherished in different terms by the world's religions.

> The widest synthesis of perfection possible to thought is the sole effort worthy of those whose dedicated vision perceives that God dwells concealed in humanity.[31]

The conclusion of Sri Aurobindo's philosophy enlists the same observation with which Spinoza concluded his *Ethics*: "But all things excellent are as difficult as they are rare."[32]

Conscious of the difficulties involved in bringing about this "big change," Sri Aurobindo's disciples, both at the Sri Aurobindo Ashram and around the world, are practicing

Integral Yoga and working for spiritual evolution according to his example and his teachings.

SRI AUROBINDO'S LEGACY

By referring to "the national aspect" of physical education, and by comparing his program for India and for the Ashram to the ideals of the Greek city-state, Sri Aurobindo points to the fact that his philosophy of Integral Yoga culminates in a kind of Indian *paideia*. In a sense, the Sri Aurobindo Ashram is intended to serve as a model primarily for Indian cultural ideals, and ultimately as a model for the universal community of man. Since Sri Aurobindo's Integral Yoga concerns the historical process as well as the individual seeker, it is only logical that the Ashram that formed around him has served as the ideal of a human community. The teachings of Sri Aurobindo and the Mother (Mira Richard, a French woman who worked closely with Sri Aurobindo since 1914, and has had complete charge of the Ashram since 1926) serve as the guide and inspiration of the entire community. Following the kind of Ashram prevalent during the Vedic period (and in contrast to most contemporary Indian Ashrams), the ideal of the Sri Aurobindo Ashram is spiritual aspiration rather than asceticism.[33]

The exact mode of this spiritual aspiration was most perfectly expressed by the Mother of the Ashram in an essay entitled "A Dream":

> There should be somewhere upon earth a place that no nation could claim as its sole property, a place where all human beings of good will, sincere in their aspirations, could live freely as citizens of the world, obeying one single authority, that of the supreme Truth, a place of peace, concord, harmony, where all the fighting instincts of man would be used exclusively to conquer the causes of his sufferings and miseries, to surmount his weakness and ignorance, to triumph over his limitations. and incapacities; a place where the needs of the spirit and the care for progress would get precedence over the satisfaction of desires and passions, the seeking for material pleasures and enjoyment. In this place, children would be able to grow and develop integrally without

losing contact with their soul. Education would be given not with a view to passing examinations and getting certificates and posts but for enriching the existing facilities and bringing forth new ones. In this place titles and positions would be supplanted by opportunities to serve and organize. The needs of the body will be provided for equally in the case of each and everyone. In the general organization intellectual, moral, and spiritual superiority will find expression not in the enhancement of the pleasures and powers of life but in the increase of duties and responsibilities. Artistic beauty in all forms, painting, sculpture, music, literature, will be available equally to all, the opportunity to share in the joys they give being limited solely by each one's capacities and not by social or financial position. For in this ideal place money would be no more the sovereign lord. Individual value would have a greater importance than the value due to material wealth and social position. Work would not be there as the means for gaining one's livelihood, it would be the means whereby to express oneself, develop one's capacities and possibilities, while doing at the same time service to the whole group, which on its side, would provide for each one's subsistence and for the field of his work. In brief, it would be a place where the relations among human beings, usually based exclusively upon competition and strife, would be replaced by relations of emulation for doing better, for collaboration, relations of real brotherhood.

The earth is certainly not ready to realize such an ideal, for mankind does not yet possess the necessary knowledge to understand and accept it or the indispensable conscious force to execute it. That is why I call it a dream.

Yet, this dream is on the way to becoming a reality. That is exactly what we are seeking to do at the Ashram of Sri Aurobindo on a small scale, in proportion to our modest means. The achievement is indeed far from being perfect but it is progressive; little by little we advance toward our goal, which, we hope, one day we shall be able to hold before the world as a practical and effective means of coming out of the present chaos in order to be born into a more true, more harmonious new life.[34]

As her extraordinary vision, writings, and directives attest, the Mother of the Sri Aurobindo Ashram is uniquely responsible for transforming this dream into a reality. The Mother's singular importance, furthermore, transcends the Ashram. As Sri Aurobindo repeatedly explains:

> The Mother's consciousness and mine are the same, the one Divine Consciousness in two, because that is necessary for the play. Nothing can be done without her knowledge and force, without her consciousness-if anybody really feels her consciousness, he should know that I am there behind it and if he feels me it is the same with hers.[35]

Sri Aurobindo identifies the Mother of the Ashram with the Divine Mother, the superconscient or supramental divine Conscious Force. In view of this identification, the Mother's responsibility of the spiritual and material welfare of the Ashram is cast in a new light. It helps to explain, for example, why the disciples follow the Mother's directives with such remarkable confidence and enthusiasm. The Ashramites accept Sri Aurobindo's mandate: "The arrangement I have made for all the disciples without exception that they should receive the light and force from her and not directly from me and be guided by her in their spiritual progress."[36] The guidance that the Mother has provided during the past four and a half decades has extended from the individual sadhana (Yoga practice) of each disciple to the governance of a community of several thousand people and their varied activities. The physical education program (concerning which Sri Aurobindo wrote *The Mind of Light*) is typical of the activities organized by the burgeoning Sri Aurobindo International Centre of Education. Other activities of the Ashram include housing and food services, workshops, scientific farming, and agriculture, a publication department and printing press, and many other creative endeavors connected with life in this spiritual-industrial, East-West community.

By far the most ambitious undertaking of the Mother and the Ashram is the creation of Auroville—"the city of human unity and universal culture" being built a few miles from the Ashram. Auroville was formally inaugurated on February 28, 1968, when students from 120 countries symbolically poured earth from their respective lands into a lotus-shaped foundation stone. This ceremony well expressed the ideals that the Mother set forth in Auroville's Charter:

> Auroville belongs to nobody in particular.
>
> Auroville belongs to humanity as a whole. But to live in Auroville one must be the willing servitor of the divine's consciousness.
>
> Auroville will be the place of an unending education, of constant progress, and a youth that never ages.
>
> Auroville wants to be the bridge between the past and the future, taking advantage of all discoveries from without and from within. Auroville will boldly spring toward future realizations.
>
> Auroville will be a site of material and spiritual research for a living embodiment of actual human unity.[37]

The name "Auroville" signifies the fact that this city is the concrete and evolving expression of Sri Aurobindo's vision of the Divine Life on earth. "Auroville" has a second, equally important meaning: it is the city of dawn, of eternal beginning.

ROBERT A. MCDERMOTT

[1] *The Life Divine*, p. 828. Unless otherwise stated, books cited in this Introduction are published by the Sri Aurobindo Ashram Press, Pondicherry, South India. The main works of Sri Aurobindo are available in US editions by Lotus Press.

[2] *Sri Aurobindo and His Ashram*, p. 6.

[3] Haridas and Uma Mukherjee, *Sri Aurobindo and The New Thought in Indian Politics* (Calcutta: Firma K. C. Mukhipadhyay, 1964), p. 219; "Politics and Spirituality," *Bande Mataram*, November 9, 1907.

[4] *Ibid.*, p. 324; "Spirituality and Nationalism," *Bande Mataram*, March 28, 1908.

[5] *Sri Aurobindo and His Ashram*, p. 41.

[6] This account of Sri Aurobindo's early life follows his own account in *Sri Aurobindo on Himself and on The Mother, Sri Aurobindo and His Ashram*, and Purani's *The Life of Sri Aurobindo*; for more complete references, see the bibliography below.

[7] *Sri Aurobindo on Himself and on The Mother*, p. 84.

[8] *Sri Aurobindo and His Ashram*, pp. 35-36.

[9] *Ibid.*, p. 36.

[10] Uttarpara Speech, in *Speeches*, p. 55.

[11] *Sri Aurobindo and His Ashram*, pp. 30-31. On two occasions Sri Aurobindo actively participated in world affairs: he publicly supported the Allied Forces against Nazi Germany, and he encouraged the Indian Nationalist leaders to accept the Cripps Offer. (*Ibid.*, p. 32)

[12] *The Life Divine*, pp. 734-735.

[13] "The Message of Sri Aurobindo," in *Sri Aurobindo and His Ashram*, p. 81.

[14] *The Life Divine*, p. 833.

[15] Nolini Kanta Gupta, "The Message of Sri Aurobindo," in *Sri Aurobindo and His Ashram*, pp. 82-83.

[16] See, for example, works by Henri Bergson, Pierre Teilhard de Chardin, and Haridas Chaudhari listed in the bibliography below.

[17] *The Life Divine*, p. 818.

[18] *Ibid.*, p. 736.

[19] In various ways, Integral Yoga draws from Patanjali's *Rajayoga, jñana-yoga* (Yoga of knowledge), *karma-yoga* (Yoga of work or selfless action), *bhakti-yoga* (the Yoga of devotion), and *dhyana-yoga* (the Yoga of meditation). According to some scholars (e.g., Ernest Wood), these Yogas are all classified as *Rajayoga* in contrast to *Hathayoga*, which is primarily physical. All *Rajayogas* are characterized by *vairagya* (nonattachment) and *abhyasa* (increasing practice). See Patanjali, *Yoga-Sutras*, sutras 8-12, and K. S. Joshi, "On the Meaning of Yoga," *Philosophy East and West*, XV (January, 1955), pp. 53-64.

[20] *The Synthesis of Yoga*, p. 504.

[21] *Ibid.*, p. 31.

[22] *Ibid.*, p. 32.

[23] *Ibid.*, p. 33. For the creative interplay of *jñana, karma,* and *bhakti* yogas, see *The Bhagavadgita* and Sri Aurobindo's *Essays on The Gita*.

[24] *Ibid.*, p. 35.

[25] *Ibid.*, p. 574.

[26] *Ibid.*, p. 576.

[27] *Ibid.*, p. 37.

[28] *Ibid.*, p. 36.

[29] *Ibid.*, p. 729.

[30] *Ibid.*, p. 492.

[31] *Ibid.*, p. 42.

[32] The last line of Spinoza's *Ethics*; see also the same observation in Plato's discussion of the philosopher-king, *Republic*, VI, 497.

[33] *Sri Aurobindo and His Ashram*, p. 48.

[34] *Ibid.*, p. 72-73.

[35] *Sri Aurobindo and His Ashram*, p. 65. For Sri Aurobindo's detailed account of the role of the Mother in human and cosmic evolution, see the third part of *Sri Aurobindo on Himself and on The Mother* (1953), and his little essay, *The Mother* (1928, reprinted 1969).

[36] *Ibid.*, p. 65

[37] *Auroville*, p. 3.

THE TEACHING OF SRI AUROBINDO

By Sri Aurobindo

The teaching of Sri Aurobindo starts from that of the ancient sages of India: that behind the appearances of the universe there is the reality of a being and consciousness, a self of all things, one and eternal. All beings are united in that one self and spirit but divided by a certain separativity of consciousness, an ignorance of their true self and reality in the mind, life and body. It is possible by a certain psychological discipline to remove this veil of separative consciousness and become aware of the true Self, the divinity within us and all.

Sri Aurobindo's teaching states that this one being and consciousness is involved here in matter. Evolution is the process by which it liberates itself; consciousness appears in what seems to be inconscient, and once having appeared is self-impelled to grow higher and higher and at the same time to enlarge and develop toward a greater and greater perfection. Life is the first step of this release of consciousness; mind is the second. But the evolution does not finish with mind; it awaits a release into something greater, a consciousness which is spiritual and supramental. The next step of the evolution must be toward the development of Supermind and spirit as the dominant power in the conscious being. For only then will the involved divinity in things release itself entirely and it become possible for life to manifest perfection.

But while the former steps in evolution were taken by nature without a conscious will in the plant and animal life, in man nature becomes able to evolve by a conscious will in the instrument. It is not, however, by the mental will in man that this can be wholly done, for the mind goes only to a certain point and after that can only move in a circle. A conversion has to be made, a turning of the consciousness by which mind has to change into the higher principle. This method is to be found through the ancient psychological discipline and practice of yoga. In the past, it has been attempted by a drawing away from the world and a disappearance into the height of the self or spirit. Sri Aurobindo teaches that a descent of the higher principle is possible which will not merely release the spiritual Self out of the world, but release it in the world, replace the mind's ignorance or its very limited knowledge by a supramental Truth-Consciousness which will be a sufficient instrument of the inner self, and make it possible for the human being to find himself dynamically as well as inwardly and grow out of his still animal humanity into a diviner race. The psychological discipline of yoga can be used to that end by opening all the parts of the being to a conversion or transformation through the descent and working of the higher, still-concealed supramental principle.

This, however, cannot be done at once or in a short time or by any rapid or miraculous transformation. Many steps have to be taken by the seeker before the supramental descent is possible. Man lives mostly in his surface mind, life, and body, but there is an inner being within him with greater possibilities to which he has to awake-for it is only a very restricted influence from it that he receives now and that pushes him to a constant pursuit of a greater beauty, harmony, power, and knowledge. The first process of yoga is therefore to open the ranges of this inner being and to live from there outward, governing his outward life by an inner light and force. In doing so he discovers in himself his true soul, which is not this outer mixture of mental, vital, and physical elements, but something of the reality behind them, a spark from the one divine fire. He has to learn to live in his soul and purify and orientate by its drive toward the truth the rest of the nature. There can follow afterwards an opening upward and descent of a higher principle of the being. But even then it is not at once the full supramental light and force. For there are several ranges of consciousness between the ordinary human mind and the supramental Truth-Consciousness. These intervening ranges have to be opened up and their power brought down into the mind, life, and body. Only afterwards can the full power of the Truth-Consciousness work in the nature. The process of this self-discipline or sadhana is therefore long and difficult, but even a little of it is so much gained because it makes the ultimate release and perfection more possible.

There are many things belonging to older systems that are necessary on the way-an opening of the mind to a greater wideness and to the sense of the self and the infinite, an emergence into what has been called the cosmic consciousness, mastery over the desires and passions; an outward asceticism is not essential, but the conquest of desire and attachment and control over the body and its needs, greeds, and instincts are indispensable. There is a combination of the principles of the old systems, the way of knowledge through the mind's discernment between reality and the appearance; the heart's way of devotion, love, and surrender; and the way of works, turning the will away from motives of self-interest to the truth and the service of a greater reality than the ego. For the whole being has to be trained so that it can respond and be transformed when it is possible for that greater light and force to work in the nature.

In this discipline the inspiration of the master and, in the difficult stages, his control and his presence are indispensable-for it would be impossible otherwise to go through it without much stumbling and error which would prevent all chance of success. The master is one who has risen to a higher consciousness and being and he is often regarded as its manifestation or representative. He not only helps by his teaching and still more by his influence and example, but by a power to communicate his own experience to others.

This is Sri Aurobindo's teaching and method of practice. It is not his object to develop any one religion or to amalgamate the older religions or to found any new religion-for any of these things would lead away from his central purpose. The one aim of his yoga is an inner self-development by which each one who follows it can in time discover the One Self in all and evolve a higher consciousness than the mental, a spiritual and supramental consciousness which will transform and divinize human nature.

MESSAGE

I take the opportunity of the publication of this issue of the "Bulletin d'Éducation Physique" of the Ashram to give my blessings to the Journal and the Association—J.S.A.S.A. (Jeunesse Sportive de l'Ashram de Sri Aurobindo). In doing so I would like to dwell for a while on the deeper *raison d'être* of such Associations and especially the need and utility for the nation of a widespread organisation of them and such sports or physical exercises as are practised here.

In their more superficial aspect they appear merely as games and amusements which people take up for entertainment or as a field for the outlet of the body's energy and natural instinct of activity or for a means of the development and maintenance of the health and strength of the body; but they are or can be much more than that: they are also fields for the development of habits, capacities and qualities which are greatly needed and of the utmost service to a people in war or in peace, and in its political and social activities, in most indeed of the provinces of a combined human endeavour. It is to this which we may call the national aspect of the subject that I would wish to give especial prominence.

In our own time these sports, games and athletics have assumed a place and command a general interest such as was seen only in earlier times in countries like Greece, Greece where all sides of human activity were equally developed and the gymnasium, chariot-racing and other sports and athletics had the same importance on the physical side as on the mental side the Arts and poetry and the drama, and were especially stimulated and attended to by the civic authorities of the city state. It was Greece that made an institution of the Olympiad and the recent re-establishment of the Olympiad as an international institution is a significant sign of the revival of the ancient spirit. This kind of interest has spread to a certain extent to our own country and India has begun to take a place in international contests such as the Olympiad. The newly founded State in liberated India is also beginning to be interested in developing all sides of the life of the nation and is likely to take an active part and a habit of direction in fields which were formerly left to private initiative. It is taking up, for instance, the question of the foundation and preservation of health and physical fitness in the nation and the spreading of a general recognition of its importance. It is in this connection that the encouragement of sports and associations for athletics and all activities of this kind would be an incalculable assistance. A generalisation of the habit of taking part in such exercises in childhood and youth and early manhood would help greatly towards the creation of a physically fit and energetic people.

But of a higher import than the foundation, however necessary, of health, strength and fitness of the body is the development of discipline and morale and sound and strong character towards which these activities can help. There are many sports which are of the utmost value towards this end, because they help to form and even necessitate the qualities of courage, hardihood, energetic action and initiative or call for skill, steadiness of will or rapid decision and action, the perception of what is to be done in an emergency and dexterity in doing it. One development of the utmost value is the awakening of the essential and instinctive body consciousness which can see and do what is necessary without any indication from mental thought and which is equivalent in the body to swift insight in the mind and spontaneous and rapid decision in the will. One may add the formation of a capacity for harmonious and right movements of the body, especially in a combined action, economical of physical effort and discouraging waste of energy, which result from such exercises as marches or drill and which displace the loose and straggling, the inharmonious or disorderly or wasteful movements common to the untrained individual body. Another invaluable result of these activities is the growth of what has been called the sporting spirit. That includes good humour and tolerance and consideration for all, a right attitude and friendliness to competitors and rivals, self-control and scrupulous observance of the laws of the game, fair play and avoidance of the use of foul means, an equal acceptance of victory or defeat without bad humour, resentment or ill-will towards successful competitors, loyal acceptance of the decisions of the appointed judge, umpire or referee. These qualities have their value for life in general and not only for sport, but the help that sport can give to their development is direct and invaluable. If they could be made more common not only in the life of the individual but in the national life and in the international where at the present day the opposite tendencies have become too rampant, existence in this troubled world of ours would be smoother and might open to a greater chance of concord and amity of which it stands very much in need. More important still is the custom of discipline, obedience, order, habit of team-work, which certain games necessitate. For without them success is uncertain or impossible. Innumerable are the activities in life, especially in national life, in which leadership and obedience to leadership in combined action are necessary for success, victory in combat or fulfillment of a purpose. The role of the leader, the captain, the power and skill of his leadership, his ability to command the confidence and ready obedience of his followers is of the utmost importance in all kinds of combined action or enterprise; but few can develop these things without having learned themselves to obey and to act as one mind or as one body with others. This strictness of training, this habit of discipline and obedience is not inconsistent with individual freedom; it is often the necessary condition for its right use, just as order is not inconsistent with liberty but rather the condition for the right use of liberty and even for its preservation and survival. In all kinds of concerted action this rule is indispensable: orchestration becomes necessary and there could be no success for an orchestra in which individual musicians played according to their own fancy and refused to follow the indications of the conductor. In spiritual things also the same rule holds; a *sadhak* who disregarded the guidance of the Guru and preferred the untrained inspirations of the novice could hardly escape the stumbles or even the disasters which so often lie thick around the path to spiritual realisation.

I need not enumerate the other benefits which can be drawn from the training that sports can give or dwell on their use in the national life; what I have said is sufficient. At any rate, in schools like ours and in universities sports have now a recognised and indispensable place; for even a highest and completest education of the mind is not enough without the education of the body. Where the qualities I have enumerated are absent or insufficiently present, a strong individual will or a national will may build them up, but the aid given by sports to their development is direct and in no way negligible. This would be a sufficient reason for the attention given to them in our Ashram, though there are others which I need not mention here. I am concerned here with their importance and the necessity of the qualities they create or stimulate for our national life. The nation which possesses them in the highest degree is likely to be the strongest for victory, success and greatness, but also for the contribution it can make towards the bringing about of unity and a more harmonious world order towards which we look as our hope for humanity's future

PERFECTION OF THE BODY

The perfection of the body, as great a perfection as we can bring about by the means at our disposal, must be the ultimate aim of physical culture. Perfection is the true aim of all culture, the spiritual and psychic, the mental, the vital and it must be the aim of our physical culture also. If our seeking is for a total perfection of the being, the physical part of it cannot be left aside; for the body is the material basis, the body is the instrument which we have to use. *Shariram khalu dharmasadhanam*, says the old Sanskrit adage—the body is the means of fulfillment of dharma, and dharma means every ideal which we can propose to ourselves and the law of its working out and its action. A total perfection is the ultimate aim which we set before us, for our ideal is the Divine Life which we wish to create here, the life of the Spirit fulfilled on earth, life accomplishing its own spiritual transformation even here on earth in the conditions of the material universe. That cannot be unless the body too undergoes a transformation, unless its action and functioning attain to a supreme capacity and the perfection which is possible to it or which can be made possible.

I have already indicated in a previous message a relative perfection of the physical consciousness in the body and of the mind, the life, the character which it houses as, no less than an awakening and development of the body's own native capacities, a desirable outcome of the exercises and practices of the physical culture to which we have commenced to give in this Ashram a special attention and scope. A development of the physical consciousness must always be a considerable part of our aim, but for that the right development of the body itself is an essential element; health, strength, fitness are the first needs, but the physical frame itself must be the best possible. A divine life in a material world implies necessarily a union of the two ends of existence, the spiritual summit and the material base. The soul with the basis of its life established in Matter ascends to the heights of the Spirit but does not cast away its base, it joins the heights and the depths together. The Spirit descends into Matter and the material world with all its lights and glories and powers and with them fills and transforms life in the material world so that it becomes more and more divine. The transformation is not a change into something purely subtle and spiritual to which Matter is in its nature repugnant and by which it is felt as an obstacle or as a shackle binding the Spirit; it takes up Matter as a form of the Spirit though now a form which conceals and turns it into a revealing instrument, it does not cast away the energies of Matter, its capacities, its methods; it brings out their hidden possibilities, uplifts, sublimates, discloses their innate divinity. The divine life will reject nothing that is capable of divinisation; all is to be seized, exalted, made utterly perfect. The mind now still ignorant, though struggling towards knowledge, has to rise towards and into the supramental light and truth and bring it down so that it shall suffuse our thinking and perception and insight and all our means of knowing till they become radiant with the highest truth in their inmost and outermost movements. Our life, still full of obscurity and confusion and occupied with so many dull and lower aims, must feel all its urges and instincts exalted and irradiated and become a glorious counterpart of the supramental super-life above. The physical consciousness and physical being, the body itself must reach a perfection in all that it is and does which now we can hardly conceive. It may even in the end be suffused with a light and beauty and bliss from the Beyond and the life divine assume a body divine.

But first the evolution of the nature must have reached a point at which it can meet the Spirit direct, feel the aspiration towards the spiritual change and open itself to the workings of the Power which shall transform it. A supreme perfection, a total perfection is possible only by a transformation of our lower or human nature, a transformation of the mind into a thing of light, our life into a thing of power, an instrument of right action, right use for all its forces, of a happy elevation of its being lifting it beyond its present comparatively narrow potentiality for a self-fulfilling force of action and joy of life. There must be equally a transforming change of the body by a conversion of its action, its functioning, its capacities as an instrument beyond the limitations by which it is clogged and hampered even in its greatest present human attainment. In the totality of the change we have to achieve, human means and forces too have to be taken up, not dropped but used and magnified to their utmost possibility as part of the new life.

Such a sublimation of our present human powers of mind and life into elements of a divine life on earth can be conceived without much difficulty; but in what figure shall we conceive the perfection of the body? In the past the body has been regarded by spiritual seekers rather as an obstacle, as something to be overcome and discarded than as an instrument of spiritual perfection and a field of the spiritual change. It has been condemned as a grossness of Matter, as an insuperable impediment and the limitations of the body as something unchangeable making transformation impossible. This is because the human body even at its best seems only to be driven by an energy of life which has its own limits and is debased in its smaller physical activities by much that is petty or coarse or evil; the body in itself is burdened with the inertia and inconscience of Matter, only partly awake and, although quickened and animated by a nervous activity, subconscient in the fundamental action of its constituent cells and tissues and their secret workings. Even in its fullest strength and force and greatest glory of beauty, it is still a flower of the material Inconscience; the inconscient is the soil from which it has grown and at every point opposes a narrow boundary to the extension of its powers and to any effort of radical self-exceeding. But if a divine life is possible on earth, then this self-exceeding must also be possible.

In the pursuit of perfection we can start at either end of our range of being and we have then to use, initially at least, the means and processes proper to our choice. In Yoga the process is spiritual and psychic; even its vital and physical processes are given a spiritual or psychic turn and raised to a higher motion than belongs properly to the ordinary life and Matter, as for instance in the Hathayogic and Rajayogic use of the breathing or the use of Asana. Ordinarily a previous preparation of the mind and life and body is necessary to make them fit for the reception of the spiritual energy and the organisation of psychic forces and methods, but this too is given a special turn proper to the Yoga. On the other hand, if we start in any field at the lower end we have to employ the means and processes which Life and Matter offer to us and respect the conditions and what we may call the technique imposed by the vital and the material energy. We may extend the activity, the achievement, the perfection attained beyond the initial, even beyond the normal possibilities but still we have to stand on the same base with which we started and within the boundaries it gives to us. It is not that the action from the two ends cannot meet and the higher take into itself and uplift the lower perfection; but this can usually be done only by a transition from the lower to a higher outlook, aspiration and motive: this we shall have to do if our aim is to transform the human into the divine life. But here there comes in the necessity of taking up the activities of human life and sublimating them by the power of the spirit. Here the lower perfection will not disappear; it will remain but will be enlarged and transformed by the higher perfection which only the power of the spirit can give. This will be evident if we consider poetry and art, philosophic thought, the perfection of the written word or the perfect organisation of earthly life: these have to be taken up and the possibilities already achieved or whatever perfection has already been attained included in a new and greater perfection but with the larger vision and inspiration of a spiritual consciousness and with new forms and powers. It must be the same with the perfection of the body.

The taking up of life and Matter into what is essentially a spiritual seeking, instead of the rejection and ultimate exclusion of them which was the attitude of a spirituality that shunned or turned away from life in the world, involves certain developments which a spiritual institution of the older kind could regard as foreign to its purpose. A divine life in the world or an institution having that for its aim and purpose cannot be or cannot remain something outside or entirely shut away from the life of ordinary men in the world or unconcerned with the mundane existence; it has to do the work of the Divine in the world and not a work outside or separate from it. The life of the ancient Rishis in their Ashramas had such a connection; they were creators, educators, guides of men and the life of the Indian people in ancient times was largely developed and directed by their shaping influence. The life and activities involved in the new endeavour are not identical but they too must be an action upon the world and a new creation in it. It must have contacts and connections with it and activities which take their place in the general life and whose initial or primary objects may not seem to differ from those of the same activities in the outside world. In our Ashram here we have found it necessary to establish a school for the education of the children of the resident *sadhaks*, teaching upon familiar lines though with certain modifications and taking as part and an important part of their development an intensive physical training which has given form to the sports and athletics practised by the Jeunesse Sportive of the Ashram and of which this Bulletin is the expression. It has been questioned by some what place sports can have in an Ashram created for spiritual seekers and what connection there can be between spirituality and sports. The first answer lies in what I have already written about the connections of an institution of this kind with the activities of the general life of men and what I have indicated in the previous number as to the utility such a training can have for the life of a nation and its benefit for the international life. Another answer can occur to us if we look beyond first objects and turn to the aspiration for a total perfection including the perfection of the body.

In the admission of an activity such as sports and physical exercises into the life of the Ashram it is evident that the methods and the first objects to be attained must belong to what we have called the lower end of the being. Originally they have been introduced for the physical education and bodily development of the children of the Ashram School, and these are too young for a strictly spiritual aim or practice to enter into their activities and it is not certain that any great number of them will enter the spiritual life when they are of an age to choose what shall be the direction of their future. The object must be the training of the body and the development of certain parts of mind and character so far as this can be done by or in connection with this training, and I have already indicated in a previous number how and in what directions this can be done. It is a relative and human perfection that can be attained within these limits; anything greater can be reached only by the intervention of higher powers, psychic powers, the power of the spirit. Yet what can be attained within the human boundaries can be something very considerable and sometimes immense: what we call genius is part of the development of the human range of being, and its achievements, especially in things of the mind and will, can carry us half-way to the divine. Even what the mind and will can do with the body in the field proper to the body and its life, in the way of physical achievement, bodily endurance, feats of prowess of all kinds, a lasting activity refusing fatigue or collapse and continuing beyond what seems at first to be possible, courage and refusal to succumb under an endless and murderous physical suffering, these and other victories of many kinds sometimes approaching or reaching the miraculous are seen in the human field and must be reckoned as a part of our concept of a total perfection. The unflinching and persistent reply that can be made by the body as well as the mind of man and by his life-energy to whatever call can be imposed on it in the most difficult and discouraging circumstances by the necessities of war and travel and adventure is of the same kind, and their endurance can reach astounding proportions and even the inconscient in the body seems to be able to return a surprising response.

The body, we have said, is a creation of the Inconscient and itself inconscient or at least subconscient in parts of itself and much of its hidden action; but what we call the Inconscient is an appearance, a dwelling place, an instrument of a secret Consciousness or a Superconscient which has created the miracle we call the universe. Matter is the field and the creation of the Inconscient and the perfection of the operations of inconscient Matter, their perfect adaptation of means to an aim and end, the wonders they perform and the marvels of beauty they create, testify, in spite of all the ignorant denial we can oppose, to the presence and power of consciousness of this Superconscience in every part and movement of the material universe. It is there in the body, has made it and its emergence in our consciousness is the secret aim of evolution and the key to the mystery of our existence.

In the use of such activities as sports and physical exercises for the education of the individual in childhood and first youth, which should mean the bringing out of his actual and latent possibilities to their fullest development, the means and methods we must use are limited by the nature of the body and its aim must be such relative human perfection of the body's powers and capacities and the powers of mind, will, character, action of which it is at once the residence and the instrument so far as these methods can help to develop them. I have written sufficiently about the mental and moral parts of perfection to which these pursuits can contribute and this I need not repeat here. For the body itself the perfections that can be developed by these means are those of its natural qualities and capacities and, secondly, the training of its general fitness as an instrument for all the activities which may be demanded from it by the mind and the will, by the life-energy or by the dynamic perceptions, impulses and instincts of our subtle physical being which is an unrecognised but very important element and agent in our nature. Health and strength are the first conditions for the natural perfection of the body, not only muscular strength and the solid strength of the limbs and physical stamina, but the finer, alert and plastic and adaptable force which our nervous and subtle physical parts can put into the activities of the frame. There is also the still more dynamic force which a call upon the life-energies can bring into the body and stir it to greater activities, even feats of the most extraordinary character of which in its normal state it would not be capable. There is also the strength which the mind and will by their demands and stimulus and by their secret powers which we use or by which we are used without knowing clearly the source of their action can impart to the body or impose upon it as masters and inspirers.

Among the natural qualities and powers of the body which can be thus awakened, stimulated and trained to a normal activity we must reckon dexterity and stability in all kinds of physical action, such as swiftness in the race, dexterity in combat, skill and endurance of the mountaineer, the constant and often extraordinary response to all that can be demanded from the body of the soldier, sailor, traveler or explorer to which I have already made reference, or in adventure of all kinds and all the wide range of physical attainment to which man has accustomed himself or to which he is exceptionally pushed by his own will or by the compulsion of circumstance. It is a general fitness of the body for all that can be asked from it which is the common formula of all this action, a fitness attained by a few or by many, that could be generalised by an extended and many-sided physical education and discipline. Some of these activities can be included under the name of sports; there are others for which sports and physical exercises can be an effective preparation. In some of them a training for common action, combined movement, discipline are needed and for that our physical exercises can make one ready; in others a developed individual will, skill of mind and quick perception, forcefulness of life-energy and subtle physical impulsion are more prominently needed and may even be the one sufficient trainer. All must be included in our conception of the natural powers of the body and its capacity and instrumental fitness in the service of the human mind and will, and therefore in our concept of the total perfection of the body.

There are two conditions for this perfection, an awakening in as great an entirety as possible of the body consciousness and an education, an evocation of its potentialities, also as entire and fully developed and, it may be, as many-sided as possible. The form or body is, no doubt, in its origin a creation of the Inconscient and limited by it on all sides, but still of the Inconscient developing the secret consciousness concealed within it and growing in light of knowledge, power and *Ananda*. We have to take it at the point it has reached in its human evolution in these things, make as full a use of them as may be and, as much as we can, further this evolution to as high a degree as is permitted by the force of the individual temperament and nature. In all forms in the world there is a force at work, unconsciously active or oppressed by inertia in its lower formulations, but in the human being conscious from the first, with its potentialities partly awake, partly asleep or latent: what is awake in it we have to make fully conscious; what is asleep we have to arouse and set to its work; what is latent we have to evoke and educate. Here there are two aspects of the body consciousness, one which seems to be a kind of automatism carrying on its work in the physical plane without any intervention of the mind and in parts even beyond any possibility of direct observation by the mind or, if conscious or observable, still proceeding or capable of continuing, when once started, by an apparently mechanical action not needing direction by the mind and continuing so long as the mind does not intervene.

There are other movements taught and trained by the mind which can yet go on operating automatically but faultlessly even when not attended to by the thought or will; there are others which can operate in sleep and produce results of value to the waking intelligence. But more important is what may be described as a trained and developed automatism, a perfected skill and capacity of eye and ear and the hands and all the members prompt to respond to any call made on them, a developed spontaneous operation as an instrument, a complete fitness for any demand that the mind and life-energy can make upon it. This is ordinarily the best we can achieve at the lower end, when we start from that end and limit ourselves to the means and methods which are proper to it. For more we have to turn to the mind and life-energy themselves or to the energy of the spirit and to what they can do for a greater perfection of the body. The most we can do in the physical field by physical means is necessarily insecure as well as bound by limits; even what seems a perfect health and strength of the body is precarious and can be broken down at any moment by fluctuations from within or by a strong attack or shock from outside: only by the breaking of our limitations can a higher and more enduring perfection come. One direction in which our consciousness must grow is an increasing hold from within or from above on the body and its powers and its more conscious response to the higher parts of our being. The mind pre-eminently is man; he is a mental being and his human perfection grows the more he fulfils the description of the Upanishad, a mental being, Purusha, leader of the life and the body. If the mind can take up and control the instincts and automatisms of the life-energy and the subtle physical consciousness and the body, if it can enter into them, consciously use and, as we may say, fully mentalise their instinctive or spontaneous action, the perfection of these energies, their action too become more conscious and more aware of themselves and more perfect. But it is necessary for the mind too to grow in perfection and this it can do best when it depends less on the fallible intellect of physical mind, when it is not limited even by the more orderly and accurate working of the reason and can grow in intuition and acquire a wider, deeper and closer seeing and the more luminous drive of energy of a higher intuitive will. Even within the limits of its present evolution it is difficult to measure the degree to which the mind is able to extend its control or its use of the body's powers and capacities and when the mind rises to higher powers still and pushes back its human boundaries, it becomes impossible to fix any limits: even, in certain realisations, an intervention by the will in the automatic working of the bodily organs seems to become possible.

Wherever limitations recede and in proportion as they recede, the body becomes a more plastic and responsive and in that measure a more fit and perfect instrument of the action of the spirit. In all effective and expressive activities here in the material world the cooperation of the two ends of our being is indispensable. If the body is unable whether by fatigue or by natural incapacity or any other cause to second the thought or will or is in any way irresponsive or insufficiently responsive, to that extent the action fails or falls short or becomes in some degree unsatisfying or incomplete. In what seems to be an exploit of the spirit so purely mental as the outpouring of poetic inspiration, there must be a responsive vibration of the brain and its openness as a channel for the power of the thought and vision and the light of the word that is making or breaking its way through or seeking for its perfect expression. If the brain is fatigued or dulled by any clog, either the inspiration cannot come and nothing is written or it fails and something inferior is all that can come out; or else a lower inspiration takes the place of the more luminous formulation that was striving to shape itself or the brain finds it more easy to lend itself to a less radiant stimulus or else it labours and constructs or responds to poetic artifice. Even in the most purely mental activities the fitness, readiness or perfect training of the bodily instrument is a condition indispensable. That readiness, that response too is part of the total perfection of the body.

The essential purpose and sign of the growing evolution here is the emergence of consciousness in an apparently inconscient universe, the growth of consciousness and with it growth of the light and power of the being; the development of the form and its functioning or its fitness to survive, although indispensable, is not the whole meaning or the central motive. The greater and greater awakening of consciousness and its climb to a higher and higher level and a wider extent of its vision and action is the condition of our progress towards that supreme and total perfection which is the aim of our existence. It is the condition also of the total perfection of the body. There are higher levels of the mind than any we now conceive and to these we must one day reach and rise beyond them to the heights of a greater, a spiritual existence. As we rise we have to open to them our lower members and fill these with those superior and supreme dynamisms of light and power; the body we have to make a more and more and even entirely conscious frame and instrument, a conscious sign and seal and power of the spirit.

As it grows in this perfection, the force and extent of its dynamic action and its response and service to the spirit must increase; the control of the spirit over it also must grow and the plasticity of its functioning both in its developed and acquired parts of power and in its automatic responses down to those that are now purely organic and seem to be the movements of a mechanic inconscience. This cannot happen without a veritable transformation, and a transformation of the mind and life and very body is indeed the change to which our evolution is secretly moving and without this transformation the entire fullness of a divine life on earth cannot emerge. In this transformation the body itself can become an agent and a partner. It might indeed be possible for the spirit to achieve a considerable manifestation with only a passive and imperfectly conscious body as its last or bottommost means of material functioning, but this could not be anything perfect or complete. A fully conscious body might even discover and work out the right material method and process of a material transformation. For this, no doubt, the spirit's supreme light and power and creative joy must have manifested on the summit of the individual consciousness and sent down their fiat into the body, but still the body may take in the working out its spontaneous part of self-discovery and achievement. It would be thus a participator and agent in its own transformation and the integral transformation of the whole being; this too would be a part and a sign and evidence of the total perfection of the body.

If the emergence and growth of consciousness is the central motive of the evolution and the key to its secret purpose, then by the very nature of that evolution this growth must involve not only a wider and wider extent of its capacities, but also an ascent to a higher and higher level till it reaches the highest possible. For it starts from a nethermost level of involution in the Inconscience which we see at work in Matter creating the material universe; it proceeds by an Ignorance which is yet ever developing knowledge and reaching out to an ever greater light and ever greater organisation and efficacy of the will and harmonisation of all its own inherent and emerging powers; it must at last reach a point where it develops or acquires the complete fullness of its capacity, and that must be a state or action in which there is no longer an ignorance seeking for knowledge but Knowledge self-possessed, inherent in the being, master of its own truths and working them out with a natural vision and force that is not afflicted by limitation or error. Or if there is a limitation, it must be a self-imposed veil behind which it would keep truth back from manifestation in Time but draw it out at will and without any need of search or acquisition in the order of a right perception of things or in the just succession of that which has to be manifested in obedience to the call of Time.

This would mean an entry or approach into what might be called a truth-consciousness self-existent in which the being would be aware of its own realities and would have the inherent power to manifest them in a Time-creation in which all would be Truth following out its own unerring steps and combining its own harmonies; every thought and will and feeling and act would be spontaneously right, inspired or intuitive, moving by the light of Truth and therefore perfect. All would express inherent realities of the spirit; some fullness of the power of the spirit would be there. One would have overpassed the present limitations of mind: mind would become a seeing of the light of Truth, will a force and power of the Truth, Life a progressive fulfillment of the Truth, the body itself a conscious vessel of the Truth and part of the means of its self-effectuation and a form of its self-aware existence. It would be at least some initiation of this Truth-consciousness, some first figure and action of it that must be reached and enter into a first operation if there is to be a divine life or any full manifestation of a spiritualised consciousness in the world of Matter. Or, at the very least, such a Truth-consciousness must be in communication with our own mind and life and body, descend into touch with it, control its seeing and action, impel its motives, take hold of its forces and shape their direction and purpose. All touched by it might not be able to embody it fully, but each would give some form to it according to his spiritual temperament, inner capacity, the line of his evolution in Nature: he would reach securely the perfection of which he was immediately capable and he would be on the road to the full possession of the truth of the Spirit and of the truth of Nature.

In the workings of such a Truth-consciousness there would be a certain conscious seeing and willing automatism of the steps of its truth which would replace the infallible automatism of the inconscient or seemingly inconscient Force that has brought out of an apparent Void the miracle of an ordered universe, and this could create a new order of the manifestation of the Being in which a perfect perfection would become possible; even a supreme and total perfection would appear in the vistas of an ultimate possibility. If we could draw down this power into the material world, our agelong dreams of human perfectibility, individual perfection, the perfectibility of the race, of society, inner mastery over self and a complete mastery, governance and utilisation of the forces of Nature could see at long last a prospect of total achievement. This complete human self-fulfillment might well pass beyond limitations and be transformed into the character of a divine life. Matter after taking into itself and manifesting the power of life and the light of mind would draw down into it the superior or supreme power and light of the spirit and in an earthly body shed its parts of inconscience and become a perfectly conscious frame of the spirit. A secure completeness and stability of the health and strength of its physical tenement could be maintained by the will and force of this inhabitant; all the natural capacities of the physical frame, all powers of the physical consciousness would reach their utmost extension and be there at command and sure of their flawless action. As an instrument the body would acquire a fullness of capacity, a totality of fitness for all uses which the inhabitant would demand of it far beyond anything now possible. Even it could become a revealing vessel of a supreme beauty and bliss, - casting the beauty of the light of the spirit suffusing and radiating from it as a lamp reflects and diffuses the luminosity of its indwelling flame, carrying in itself the beatitude of the spirit, its joy of the seeing mind, its joy of life and spiritual happiness, the joy of Matter released into a spiritual consciousness and thrilled with a constant ecstasy. This would be the total perfection of the spiritualised body.

All this might not come all at once, though such a sudden illumination might be possible if a divine Power and Light and *Ananda* could take their stand on the summit of our being and send down their force into the mind and life and body illumining and remoulding the cells, awaking consciousness in all the frame. But the way would be open and the consummation of all that is possible in the individual could progressively take place. The physical also would have its share in that consummation of the whole.

There would always remain vistas beyond as the infinite

Spirit took up towards higher heights and larger breadths the evolving Nature, in the movement of the liberated being towards the possession of the supreme Reality, the supreme existence, consciousness, beatitude. But of this it would be premature to speak: what has been written is perhaps as much as the human mind as it is now constituted can venture to look forward to and the enlightened thought understand in some measure. These consequences of the Truth-consciousness descending and laying its hold upon Matter would be a sufficient justification of the evolutionary labour. In this upward all-uplifting sweep of the Spirit there could be a simultaneous or consecutive downward sweep of the triumph of a spiritualised Nature all-including, all-transmuting and in it there could occur a glorifying change of Matter and the physical consciousness and physical form and functioning of which we could speak as not only the total but the supreme perfection of the body.

THE DIVINE BODY

A divine life in a divine body is the formula of the ideal that we envisage. But what will be the divine body? What will be the nature of this body, its structure, the principle of its activity, the perfection that distinguishes it from the limited and imperfect physicality within which we are now bound? What will be the conditions and operations of its life, still physical in its base upon the earth, by which it can be known as divine? If it is to be the product of an evolution, and it is so that we must envisage it, an evolution out of our human imperfection and ignorance into a greater truth of spirit and nature, by what process or stages can it grow into manifestation or rapidly arrive? The process of the evolution upon earth has been slow and tardy - what principle must intervene if there is to be a transformation, a progressive or sudden change? It is indeed as a result of our evolution that we arrive at the possibility of this transformation. As Nature has evolved beyond Matter and manifested Life, beyond Life and manifested Mind, so she must evolve beyond Mind and manifest a consciousness and power of our existence free from the imperfection and limitation of our mental existence, a supramental or truth-consciousness, and able to develop the power and perfection of the spirit. Here a slow and tardy change need no longer be the law or manner of our evolution; it will be only so to a greater or less extent so long as a mental ignorance clings and hampers our ascent; but once we have grown into the truth-consciousness its power of spiritual truth of being will determine all. Into that truth we shall be freed and it will transform mind and life and body. Light and bliss and beauty and a perfection of the spontaneous right action of all the being are there as native powers of the supramental truth-consciousness and these will in their very nature transform mind and life and body even here upon earth into a manifestation of the truth-conscious spirit. The obscurations of earth will not prevail against the supramental truth-consciousness, for even into the earth it can bring enough of the omniscient light and omnipotent force of the spirit to conquer. All may not open to the fullness of its light and power, but whatever does open must to that extent undergo the change. That will be the principle of transformation.

It might be that a psychological change, a mastery of the nature by the soul, a transformation of the mind into a principle of light, of the life-force into power and purity would be the first approach, the first attempt to solve the problem, to escape beyond the merely human formula and establish something that could be called a divine life upon earth, a first sketch of supermanhood, of a supramental living in the circumstances of the earth-nature. But this could not be the complete and radical change needed; it would not be the total transformation, the fullness of a divine life in a divine body. There would be a body still human and indeed animal in its origin and fundamental character and this would impose its own inevitable limitations on the higher parts of the embodied being. As limitation by ignorance and error is the fundamental defect of an untransformed mind, as limitation by the imperfect impulses and strainings and wants of desire are the defects of an untransformed life-force, so also imperfection of the potentialities of the physical action, an imperfection, a limitation in the response of its half-consciousness to the demands made upon it and the grossness and stains of its original animality would be the defects of an untransformed or an imperfectly transformed body. These could not but hamper and even pull down towards themselves the action of the higher parts of the nature. A transformation of the body must be the condition for a total transformation of the nature.

It might be also that the transformation might take place by stages; there are powers of the nature still belonging to the mental region which are yet potentialities of a growing gnosis lifted beyond our human mentality and partaking of the light and power of the Divine and an ascent through these planes, a descent of them into the mental being might seem to be the natural evolutionary course.

But in practice it might be found that these intermediate levels would not be sufficient for the total transformation since, being themselves illumined potentialities of mental being not yet supramental in the full sense of the word, they could bring down to the mind only a partial divinity or raise the mind towards that but not effectuate its elevation into the complete supramentality of the truth-consciousness. Still these levels might become stages of the ascent which some would reach and pause there while others went higher and could reach and live on superior strata of a semi-divine existence. It is not to be supposed that all humanity would rise in a block into the Supermind; at first those only might attain to the highest or some intermediate height of the ascent whose inner evolution has fitted them for so great a change or who are raised by the direct touch of the Divine into its perfect light and power and bliss. The large mass of human beings might still remain for long content with a normal or only a partially illumined and uplifted human nature. But this would be itself a sufficiently radical change and initial transformation of earth-life; for the way would be open to all who have the will to rise, the supramental influence of the truth-consciousness would touch the earth-life and influence even its untransformed mass and a hope would be there and a promise eventually available to all which now only the few can share in or realise.

In any case these would be beginnings only and could not constitute the fullness of the divine life upon earth; it would be a new orientation of the earthly life but not the consummation of its change. For that there must be the sovereign reign of a supramental truth-consciousness to which all other forms of life would be subordinated and depend upon it as the master principle and supreme power to which they could look up as the goal, profit by its influences, be moved and upraised by something of its illumination and penetrating force. Especially, as the human body had to come into existence with its modification of the previous animal form and its erect figure of a new power of life and its expressive movements and activities serviceable and necessary to the principle of mind and the life of a mental being, so too a body must be developed with new powers, activities or degrees of a divine action expressive of a truth-conscious being and proper to a supramental consciousness and manifesting a conscious spirit. While the capacity for taking up and sublimating all the activities of the earth-life capable of being spiritualised must be there, a transcendence of the original animality and the actions incurably tainted by it or at least some saving transformation of them, some spiritualising or psychicising of the consciousness and motives animating them and the shedding of whatever could not be so transformed, even a change of what might be called its instrumental structure, its functioning and organisation, a complete and hitherto unprecedented control of these things must be the consequence or incidental to this total change. These things have been already to some extent illustrated in the lives of many who have become possessed of spiritual powers but as something exceptional and occasional, the casual or incomplete manifestation of an acquired capacity rather than the organisation of a new consciousness, a new life and a new nature. How far can such physical transformation be carried, what are the limits within which it must remain to be consistent with life upon earth and without carrying that life beyond the earthly sphere or pushing it towards the supraterrestrial existence? The supramental consciousness is not a fixed quantity but a power which passes to higher and higher levels of possibility until it reaches supreme consummations of spiritual existence fulfilling Supermind as Supermind fulfils the ranges of spiritual consciousness that are pushing towards it from the human or mental level. In this progression the body also may reach a more perfect form and a higher range of its expressive powers, become a more and more perfect vessel of divinity.

This destiny of the body has rarely in the past been envisaged or else not for the body here upon earth; such forms would rather be imagined or visioned as the privilege of celestial beings and not possible as the physical residence of a soul still bound to terrestrial nature. The Vaishnavas have spoken of a spiritualised conscious body, *chinmaya deha*; there has been the conception of a radiant or luminous body, which might be the Vedic *jyotirmaya deha*. A light has been seen by some radiating from the bodies of highly developed spiritual persons, even extending to the emission of an enveloping aura and there has been recorded an initial phenomenon of this kind in the life of so great a spiritual personality as Ramakrishna. But these things have been either conceptual only or rare and occasional and for the most part the body has not been regarded as possessed of spiritual possibility or capable of transformation. It has been spoken of as the means of effectuation of the dharma and dharma here includes all high purposes, achievements and ideals of life not excluding the spiritual change: but it is an instrument that must be dropped when its work is done and though there may be and must be spiritual realisation while yet in the body, it can only come to its full fruition after the abandonment of the physical frame. More ordinarily in the spiritual tradition the body has been regarded as an obstacle, incapable of spiritualisation or transmutation and a heavy weight holding the soul to earthly nature and preventing its ascent either to spiritual fulfillment in the Supreme or to the dissolution of its individual being in the Supreme. But while this conception of the role of the body in our destiny is suitable enough for a sadhana that sees earth only as a field of the ignorance and earth-life as a preparation for a saving withdrawal from life which is the indispensable condition for spiritual liberation, it is insufficient for a sadhana which conceives of a divine life upon earth and liberation of earth-nature itself as part of a total purpose of the embodiment of the spirit here. If a total transformation of the being is our aim, a transformation of the body must be an indispensable part of it; without that no full divine life on earth is possible.

It is the past evolution of the body and especially its animal nature and animal history which seems to stand in the way of this consummation. The body, as we have seen, is an offspring and creation of the Inconscient, itself inconscient or only half-conscious; it began as a form of unconscious Matter, developed life and from a material object became a living growth, developed mind and from the subconsciousness of the plant and the initial rudimentary mind or incomplete intelligence of the animal developed the intellectual mind and more complete intelligence of man and now serves as the physical base, container and instrumental means of our total spiritual endeavour. Its animal character and its gross limitations stand indeed as an obstacle to our spiritual perfection; but the fact that it has developed a soul and is capable of serving it as a means may indicate that it is capable of further development and may become a shrine and expression of the spirit, reveal a secret spirituality of Matter, become entirely and not only half-conscious, reach a certain oneness with the spirit. This much it must do, so far at least it must transcend its original earth-nature, if it is to be the complete instrument of the divine life and no longer an obstacle.

Still the inconveniences of the animal body and its animal
nature and impulses and the limitations of the human body
at its best are there in the beginning and persist always so
long as there is not the full and fundamental liberation, and
its inconscience or half-conscience and its binding of the soul
and mind and life-force to Matter, to materiality of all kinds,
to the call of the unregenerated earth-nature are there and
constantly oppose the call of the spirit and circumscribe the
climb to higher things. To the physical being it brings a
bondage to the material instruments, to the brain and heart
and senses, wed to materiality and materialism of all kinds,
to the bodily mechanism and its needs and obligations, to
the imperative need of food and the preoccupation with the
means of getting it and storing it as one of the besetting
interests of life, to fatigue and sleep, to the satisfaction of
bodily desire. The life-force in man also is tied down to these
small things; it has to limit the scope of its larger ambitions
and longings, its drive to rise beyond the pull of earth and
follow the heavenlier intuitions of its psychic parts, the heart's
ideal and the soul's yearnings. On the mind the body imposes
the boundaries of the physical being and the physical life
and the sense of the sole complete reality of physical things
with the rest as a sort of brilliant fireworks of the imagination,
of lights and glories that can only have their full play in
heavens beyond, on higher planes of existence, but not here;
it afflicts the idea and aspiration with the burden of doubt,
the evidence of the subtle senses and the intuition with
uncertainty and the vast field of supraphysical consciousness
and experience with the imputation of unreality and clamps
down to its earth-roots the growth of the spirit from its original
limiting humanity into the supramental truth and the divine
nature. These obstacles can be overcome, the denials and
resistance of the body surmounted, its transformation is
possible. Even the inconscient and animal part of us can be
illumined and made capable of manifesting the god-nature,
even as our mental humanity can be made to manifest the
superhumanity of the supramental Truth-Consciousness and
the divinity of what is now superconscious to us, and the
total transformation made a reality here. But for this the
obligations and compulsions of its animality must cease to
be obligatory and a purification of its materiality effected by
which that very materiality can be turned into a material

solidity of the manifestation of the divine nature. For nothing essential must be left out in the totality of the earth-change; Matter itself can be turned into a means of revelation of the spiritual reality, the Divine.

The difficulty is dual, psychological and corporeal: the first is the effect of the unregenerated animality upon the life, especially by the insistence of the body's gross instincts, impulses, desires; the second is the outcome of our corporeal structure and organic instrumentation imposing its restrictions on the dynamism of the higher divine nature. The first of these two difficulties is easier to deal with and conquer; for here the will can intervene and impose on the body the power of the higher nature. Certain of these impulses and instincts of the body have been found especially harmful by the spiritual aspirant and weighed considerably in favour of an ascetic rejection of the body. Sex and sexuality and all that springs from sex and testifies to its existence had to be banned and discarded from the spiritual life, and this, though difficult, is not at all impossible and can be made a cardinal condition for the spiritual seeker. This is natural and unescapable in all ascetic practice and the satisfaction of this condition, though not easy at first to fulfill, becomes after a time quite feasible; the overcoming of the sex instinct and impulse is indeed binding on all who would attain to self-mastery and lead the spiritual life. A total mastery over it is essential for all spiritual seekers, the eradication of it for the complete ascetic. This much has to be recognised and not diminished in its obligatory importance and its principle.

But all recognition of the sex principle, as apart from the gross physical indulgence of the sex impulse, could not be excluded from a divine life upon earth; it is there in life, plays a large part and has to be dealt with, it cannot simply be ignored, merely suppressed or held down or put away out of sight. In the first place, it is in one of its aspects a cosmic and even a divine principle: it takes the spiritual form of the *Ishwara* and the Shakti and without it there could be no world-creation or manifestation of the world-principle of Purusha and Prakriti which are both necessary for the creation, necessary too in their association and interchange for the play of its psychological working and in their manifestation as soul and Nature fundamental to the whole process of the *Lila*. In the divine life itself an incarnation or at least in some form a presence of the two powers or their initiating influence through their embodiments or representatives would be indispensable for making the new creation possible. In its human action on the mental and vital level sex is not altogether an undivine principle; it has its nobler aspects and idealities and it has to be seen in what way and to what extent these can be admitted into the new and larger life. All gross animal indulgence of sex desire and impulse would have to be eliminated; it could only continue among those who are not ready for the higher life or not yet ready for a complete spiritual living. In all who aspired to it but could not yet take it up in its fullness sex will have to be refined, submit to the spiritual or psychic impulse and a control by the higher mind and the higher vital and shed all its lighter, frivolous or degraded forms and feel the touch of the purity of the ideal. Love would remain, all forms of the pure truth of love in higher and higher steps till it realised its highest nature, widened into universal love, merged into the love of the Divine. The love of man and woman would also undergo that elevation and consummation; for all that can feel a touch of the ideal and the spiritual must follow the way of ascent till it reaches the divine Reality. The body and its activities must be accepted as part of the divine life and pass under this law; but, as in the other evolutionary transitions, what cannot accept the law of the divine life cannot be accepted and must fall away from the ascending nature.

Another difficulty that the transformation of the body has to face is its dependence for its very existence upon food, and here too are involved the gross physical instincts, impulses, desires that are associated with this difficult factor, the essential cravings of the palate, the greed of food and animal gluttony of the belly, the coarsening of the mind when it grovels in the mud of sense, obeys a servitude to its mere animal part and hugs its bondage to Matter. The higher human in us seeks refuge in a temperate moderation, in abstemiousness and abstinence or in carelessness about the body and its wants and in an absorption in higher things. The spiritual seeker often, like the Jain ascetics, seeks refuge in long and frequent fasts which lift him temporarily at least out of the clutch of the body's demands and help him to feel in himself a pure vacancy of the wide rooms of the spirit. But all this is not liberation and the question may be raised whether, not only at first but always, the divine life also must submit to this necessity. But it could only deliver itself from it altogether if it could find out the way so to draw upon the universal energy that the energy would sustain not only the vital parts of our physicality but its constituent matter with no need of aid for sustenance from any outside substance of Matter. It is indeed possible even while fasting for very long periods to maintain the full energies and activities of the soul and mind and life, even those of the body, to remain wakeful but concentrated in Yoga all the time, or to think deeply and write day and night, to dispense with sleep, to walk eight hours a day, maintaining all these activities separately or together, and not feel any loss of strength, any fatigue, any kind of failure or decadence. At the end of the fast one can even resume at once taking the normal or even a greater than the normal amount of nourishment without any transition or precaution such as medical science enjoins, as if both the complete fasting and the feasting were natural conditions, alternating by an immediate and easy passage from one to the other, of a body already trained by a sort of initial transformation to be an instrument of the powers and activities of Yoga. But one thing one does not escape and that is the wasting of the material tissues of the body, its flesh and substance. Conceivably, if a practicable way and means could only be found, this last invincible obstacle too might be overcome and the body maintained by an interchange of its forces with the forces of material Nature, giving to her her need from the individual and taking from her directly the sustaining energies of her universal existence. Conceivably, one might rediscover and re-establish at the summit of the evolution of life the phenomenon we see at its base, the power to draw from all around it the means of sustenance and self-renewal. Or else the evolved being might acquire the greater power to draw down those means from above rather than draw them up or pull them in from the environment around, all about it and below it. But until something like this is achieved or made possible we have to go back to food and the established material forces of Nature.

In fact we do, however unconsciously, draw constantly upon the universal energy, the force in Matter to replenish our material existence and the mental, vital and other potencies in the body: we do it directly in the invisible processes of interchange constantly kept up by Nature and by special means devised by her; breathing is one of these, sleep also and repose. But as her basic means for maintaining and renewing the gross physical body and its workings and inner potencies Nature has selected the taking in of outside matter in the shape of food, its digestion, assimilation of what is assimilable and elimination of what cannot or ought not to be assimilated; this by itself is sufficient for mere maintenance, but for assuring health and strength in the body so maintained it has added the impulse towards physical exercise and play of many kinds, ways for the expenditure and renewal of energy, the choice or the necessity of manifold action and labour. In the new life, in its beginnings at least, it would not be necessary or advisable to make any call for an extreme or precipitate rejection of the need of food or the established natural method for the maintenance of the still imperfectly transformed body. If or when these things have to be transcended it must come as a result of the awakened will of the spirit, a will also in Matter itself, an imperative evolutionary urge, an act of the creative transmutations of Time or a descent from the transcendence. Meanwhile the drawing in of the universal energy by a conscious action of the higher powers of the being from around or from above, by a call to what is still to us a transcending consciousness or by an invasion or descent from the Transcendence itself, may well become an occasional, a frequent or a constant phenomenon and even reduce the part played by food and its need to an incidence no longer preoccupying, a necessity minor and less and less imperative.

Meanwhile food and the ordinary process of Nature can be accepted, although its use has to be liberated from attachment and desire and the grosser undiscriminating appetites and clutch at the pleasures of the flesh which is the way of the Ignorance; the physical processes have to be subtilised and the grossest may have to be eliminated and new processes found or new instrumentalities emerge. So long as it is accepted, a refined pleasure in it may be permitted and even a desireless *ananda* of taste take the place of the physical relish and the human selection by likings and dislikings which is our present imperfect response to what is offered to us by Nature. It must be remembered that for the divine life on earth, earth and Matter have not to be and cannot be rejected but have only to be sublimated and to reveal in themselves the possibilities of the spirit, serve the spirit's highest uses and be transformed into instruments of a greater living.

The divine life must always be actuated by the push towards perfection; a perfection of the joy of life is part and an essential part of it, the body's delight in things and the body's joy of life are not excluded from it; they too have to be made perfect. A large totality is the very nature of this new and growing way of existence, a fullness of the possibilities of the mind transmuted into a thing of light, of the life converted into a force of spiritual power and joy, of the body transformed into an instrument of a divine action, divine knowledge, divine bliss.

All can be taken into its scope that is capable of transforming itself, all that can be an instrument, a vessel, an opportunity for the expression of this totality of the self-manifesting Spirit.

There is one problem raised by sex for those who would reject in toto the obligations imposed by the animality of the body and put forward by it as an insistent opposition in the way of the aspirant to a higher life: it is the necessity of the prolongation of the race for which the sex activity is the only means already provided by Nature for living beings and inevitably imposed upon the race. It is not indeed necessary for the individual seeker after a divine life to take up this problem or even for a group who do not seek after it for themselves alone but desire a wide acceptance of it by mankind as at least an ideal. There will always be the multitude who do not concern themselves with it or are not ready for its complete practice and to these can be left the care for the prolongation of the race. The number of those who lead the divine life can be maintained and increased, as the ideal extends itself, by the voluntary adhesion of those who are touched by the aspiration and there need be no resort to physical means for this purpose, no deviation from the rule of a strict sexual abstinence. But yet there may be circumstances in which, from another standpoint, a voluntary creation of bodies for souls that seek to enter the earth-life to help in the creation and extension of the divine life upon earth might be found to be desirable. Then the necessity of a physical procreation for this purpose could only be avoided if new means of a supraphysical kind were evolved and made available. A development of this kind must necessarily belong to what is now considered as the sphere of the occult and the use of concealed powers of action or creation not known or possessed by the common mind of the race. Occultism means rightly the use of the higher powers of our nature, soul, mind, life-force and the faculties of the subtle physical consciousness to bring about results on their own or on the material plane by some pressure of their own secret law and its potentialities, for manifestation and result in human or earthly mind and life and body or in objects and events in the world of Matter. A discovery or an extension of these little known or yet undeveloped powers is now envisaged by some well-known thinkers as a next step to be taken by mankind in its immediate evolution; the kind of creation spoken of has not been included among these developments, but it could well be considered as one of the new possibilities. Even physical science is trying to find physical means for passing beyond the ordinary instrumentation or procedure of Nature in this matter of propagation or the renewal of the physical life-force in human or animal beings; but the resort to occult means and the intervention of subtle physical processes, if it could be made possible, would be a greater way which could avoid the limitations, degradations, incompleteness and heavy imperfection of the means and results solely available to the law of material force.

In India there has been always from the earliest times a widely spread belief in the possibility and reality of the use of these powers by men with an advanced knowledge of these secret things or with a developed spiritual knowledge and experience and dynamic force and even, in the Tantras, an organised system of their method and practice. The intervention of the Yogi in bringing about a desired birth of offspring is also generally believed in and often appealed to and the bestowal on the child so obtained of a spiritual attainment or destiny by his will or his blessing is sometimes asked for and such a result is recorded not only in the tradition of the past but maintained by the witness of the present. But there is here still the necessity of a resort to the normal means of propagation and the gross method of physical Nature. A purely occult method, a resort to supraphysical processes acting by supraphysical means for a physical result would have to be possible if we are to avoid this necessity: the resort to the sex impulse and its animal process could not be transcended otherwise. If there is some reality in the phenomenon of materialisation and dematerialisation claimed to be possible by occultists and evidenced by occurrences many of us have witnessed, a method of this kind would not be out of the range of possibility. For in the theory of the occultists and in the gradation of the ranges and planes of our being which Yoga-knowledge outlines for us there is not only a subtle physical force but a subtle physical Matter intervening between life and gross Matter, and to create in this subtle physical substance and precipitate the forms thus made into our grosser materiality is feasible. It should be possible and it is believed to be possible for an object formed in this subtle physical substance to make a transit from its subtlety into the state of gross Matter directly by the intervention of an occult force and process, whether with or even without the assistance or intervention of some gross material procedure. A soul wishing to enter into a body or form for itself a body and take part in a divine life upon earth might be assisted to do so or even provided with such a form by this method of direct transmutation, without passing through birth by the sex process or undergoing any degradation or any of the heavy limitations in the growth and development of its mind and material body inevitable to our present way of existence. It might then assume at once the structure and greater powers and functionings of the truly divine material body which must one day emerge in a progressive evolution to a totally transformed existence both of life and form in a divinised earth-nature.

But what would be the internal or external form and structure and what the instrumentation of this divine body? The material history of the development of the animal and human body has left it bound to a minutely constructed and elaborated system of organs and a precarious order of their functioning which can easily become a disorder, open to a general or local disorganisation, dependent on an easily disturbed nervous system and commanded by a brain whose vibrations are supposed to be mechanical and automatic and not under our conscious control. According to the materialist all this is a functioning of Matter alone whose fundamental reality is chemical. We have to suppose that the body is constructed by the agency of chemical elements building up atoms and molecules and cells and these again are the agents and only conductors at the basis of a complicated physical structure and instrumentation which is the sole mechanical cause of all our actions, thoughts, feelings, the soul a fiction and mind and life only a material and mechanical manifestation and appearance of this machine which is worked out and automatically driven with a figment of consciousness in it by the forces inherent in inconscient Matter. If that were the truth it is obvious that any divinisation or divine transformation of the body or of anything else would be nothing but an illusion, an imagination, a senseless and impossible chimera. But even if we suppose a soul, a conscious will at work in this body it could not arrive at a divine transformation if there were no radical change in the bodily instrument itself and in the organisation of its material workings. The transforming agent will be bound and stopped in its work by the physical organism's unalterable limitations and held up by the unmodified or imperfectly modified original animal in us. The possibility of the disorders, derangements, maladies native to these physical arrangements would still be there and could only be shut out by a constant vigilance or perpetual control obligatory on the corporeal instrument's spiritual inhabitant and master. This could not be called a truly divine body; for in a divine body an inherent freedom from all these things would be natural and perpetual; this freedom would be a normal and native truth of its being and therefore inevitable and unalterable. A radical transformation of the functioning and, it may well be, of the structure and certainly of the too mechanical and material impulses and driving forces of the bodily system would be imperative.

What agency could we find which we could make the means of this all-important liberation and change? Something there is in us or something has to be developed, perhaps a central and still occult part of our being containing forces whose powers in our actual and present make-up are only a fraction of what could be, but if they became complete and dominant would be truly able to bring about with the help of the light and force of the soul and the supramental truth-consciousness the necessary physical transformation and its consequences.

This might be found in the system of Chakras revealed by Tantric knowledge and accepted in the systems of Yoga, conscious centres and sources of all the dynamic powers of our being organising their action through the plexuses and arranged in an ascending series from the lowest physical to the highest mind centre and spiritual centre called the thousand-petalled lotus where ascending Nature, the Serpent Power of the Tantrics, meets the Brahman and is liberated into the Divine Being. These centres are closed or half-closed within us and have to be opened before their full potentiality can be manifested in our physical nature: but once they are opened and completely active, no limit can easily be set to the development of their potencies and the total transformation to be possible.

But what would be the result of the emergence of these forces and their liberated and diviner action on the body itself, what their dynamic connection with it and their transforming operation on the still existing animal nature and its animal impulses and gross material procedure? It might be held that the first necessary change would be the liberation of the mind, the life-force, the subtle physical agencies and the physical consciousness into a freer and a diviner activity, a many-dimensioned and unlimited operation of their consciousness, a large outbreak of higher powers and the sublimation of the bodily consciousness itself, of its instrumentation, capacity, capability for the manifestation of the soul in the world of Matter. The subtle senses now concealed in us might come forward into a free action and the material senses themselves become means or channels for the vision of what is now invisible to us or the discovery of things surrounding us but at present unseizable and held back from our knowledge. A firm check might be put on the impulses of the animal nature or they might be purified and subtilised so as to become assets and not liabilities and so transformed as to be parts and processes of a diviner life. But even these changes would still leave a residue of material processes keeping the old way and not amenable to the higher control and, if this could not be changed, the rest of the transformation might itself be checked and incomplete. A total transformation of the body would demand a sufficient change of the most material part of the organism, its constitution, its processes and its set-up of nature.

Again, it might be thought that a full control would be sufficient, a knowledge and a vision of this organism and its unseen action and an effective control determining its operations according to the conscious will; this possibility has been affirmed as something already achieved and a part of the development of the inner powers in some. The cessation of the breathing while still the life of the body remained stable, the hermetic sealing up at will not only of the breath but of all the vital manifestations for long periods, the stoppage of the heart similarly at will while thought and speech and other mental workings continued unabated, these and other phenomena of the power of the will over the body are known and well-attested examples of this kind of mastery. But these are occasional or sporadic successes and do not amount to transformation; a total control is necessary and an established and customary and, indeed, a natural mastery. Even with that achieved something more fundamental might have to be demanded for the complete liberation and change into a divine body.

Again, it might be urged that the organic structure of the body no less than its basic outer form would have to be retained as a necessary material foundation for the retention of the earth-nature, the connection of the divine life with the life of earth and a continuance of the evolutionary process so as to prevent a breaking upward out of and away from it into a state of being which would properly belong to a higher plane and not to a terrestrial divine fulfillment. The prolonged existence of the animal itself in our nature, if sufficiently transformed to be an instrument of manifestation and not an obstacle, would be necessary to preserve the continuity, the evolutionary total; it would be needed as the living vehicle, *vahana*, of the emergent god in the material world where he would have to act and achieve the works and wonders of the new life. It is certain that a form of body making this connection and a bodily action containing the earth-dynamism and its fundamental activities must be there, but the connection should not be a bond or a confining limitation or a contradiction of the totality of the change. The maintenance of the present organism without any transformation of it would not but act as such a bond and confinement within the old nature. There would be a material base but it would be of the earth earthy, an old and not a new earth with a diviner psychological structure; for with that structure the old system would be out of harmony and it would be unable to serve its further evolution or even to uphold it as a base in Matter. It would bind part of the being, a lower part to an untransformed humanity and unchanged animal functioning and prevent its liberation into the superhumanity of the supramental nature. A change is then necessary here too, a necessary part of the total bodily transformation, which would divinise the whole man, at least in the ultimate result, and not leave his evolution incomplete.

This aim, it might be said, would be sufficiently served if the instrumentation of the centres and their forces reigned over all the activities of the nature with an entire domination of the body and made it both in its structural form and its organic workings a free channel and means of communication and a plastic instrument of cognition and dynamic action for all that they had to do in the material life, in the world of Matter. There would have to be a change in the operative processes of the material organs themselves and, it may well be, in their very constitution and their importance; they could not be allowed to impose their limitations imperatively on the new physical life. To begin with, they might become more clearly outer ends of the channels of communication and action, more serviceable for the psychological purposes of the inhabitant, less blindly material in their responses, more conscious of the act and aim of the inner movements and powers which use them and which they are wrongly supposed by the material man in us to generate and to use. The brain would be a channel of communication of the form of the thoughts and a battery of their insistence on the body and the outside world where they could then become effective directly, communicating themselves without physical means from mind to mind, producing with a similar directness effects on the thoughts, actions and lives of others or even upon material things. The heart would equally be a direct communicant and medium of interchange for the feelings and emotions thrown outward upon the world by the forces of the psychic centre. Heart could reply directly to heart, the life-force come to the help of other lives and answer their call in spite of strangeness and distance, many beings without any external communication thrill with the message and meet in the secret light from one divine centre. The will might control the organs that deal with food, safeguard automatically the health, eliminate greed and desire, substitute subtler processes or draw in strength and substance from the universal life-force so that the body could maintain for a long time its own strength and substance without loss or waste, remaining thus with no need of sustenance by material aliments, and yet continue a strenuous action with no fatigue or pause for sleep or repose. The soul's will or the mind's could act from higher sources upon the sex centre and the sex organs so as to check firmly or even banish the grosser sexual impulse or stimulus and instead of serving an animal excitation or crude drive or desire turn their use to the storing, production and direction towards brain and heart and life-force of the essential energy, *ojas*, of which this region is the factory so as to support the works of the mind and soul and spirit and the higher life-powers and limit the expenditure of the energy on lower things. The soul, the psychic being, could more easily fill all with the light and turn the very matter of the body to higher uses for its own greater purpose.

This would be a first potent change, but not by any means all that is possible or desirable. For it may well be that the evolutionary urge would proceed to a change of the organs themselves in their material working and use and diminish greatly the need of their instrumentation and even of their existence. The centres in the subtle body, *sukshma sharira*, of which one would become conscious and aware of all going on in it, would pour their energies into material nerve and plexus and tissue and radiate them through the whole material body; all the physical life and its necessary activities in this new existence could be maintained and operated by these higher agencies in a freer and ampler way and by a less burdensome and restricting method. This might go so far that these organs might cease to be indispensable and even be felt as too obstructive: the central force might use them less and less and finally throw aside their use altogether. If that happened they might waste by atrophy, be reduced to an insignificant minimum or even disappear. The central force might substitute for them subtle organs of a very different character or, if anything material was needed, instruments that would be forms of dynamism or plastic transmitters rather than what we know as organs.

This might well be part of a supreme total transformation of the body, though this too might not be final. To envisage such changes is to look far ahead and minds attached to the present form of things may be unable to give credence to their possibility. No such limits and no such impossibility of any necessary change can be imposed on the evolutionary urge. All has not to be fundamentally changed: on the contrary, all has to be preserved that is still needed in the totality, but all has to be perfected. Whatever is necessary for the evolutionary purpose for the increasing, enlarging, heightening of the consciousness, which seems to be its

central will and aim here, or the progression of its enabling
means and preserving environment, has to be kept and
furthered; but what has to be overpassed, whatever has no
longer a use or is degraded, what has become unhelpful or
retarding, can be discarded and dropped on the way. That
has been evident in the history of the evolution of the body
from its beginning in elementary forms to its most developed
type, the human; there is no reason why this process should
not intervene in the transition from the human into the
divine body. For the manifestation or building of a divine
body on earth there must be an initial transformation, the
appearance of a new, a greater and more developed type, not
a continuance with little modifications of the present physical
form and its limited possibilities. What has to be preserved
must indeed be preserved and that means whatever is
necessary or thoroughly serviceable for the uses of the new
life on earth; whatever is still needed and will serve its purpose
but is imperfect, will have to be retained but developed and
perfected; whatever is no longer of use for new aims or is a
disability must be thrown aside. The necessary forms and
instrumentations of Matter must remain since it is in a world
of Matter that the divine life has to manifest, but their
materiality must be refined, uplifted, ennobled, illumined,
since Matter and the world of Matter have increasingly to
manifest the indwelling Spirit.

The new type, the divine body, must continue the already
developed evolutionary form; there must be a continuation
from the type Nature has all along been developing, a
continuity from the human to the divine body, no breaking
away to something unrecognisable but a high sequel to what
has already been achieved and in part perfected. The human
body has in it parts and instruments that have been
sufficiently evolved to serve the divine life; these have to
survive in their form, though they must be still further
perfected, their limitations of range and use removed, their
liability to defect and malady and impairment eliminated,
their capacities of cognition and dynamic action carried
beyond the present limits.

New powers have to be acquired by the body which our
present humanity could not hope to realise, could not even
dream of or could only imagine. Much that can now only be
known, worked out or created by the use of invented tools
and machinery might be achieved by the new body in its

own power or by the inhabitant spirit through its own direct spiritual force. The body itself might acquire new means and ranges of communication with other bodies, new processes of acquiring knowledge, a new aesthesis, new potencies of manipulation of itself and objects. It might not be impossible for it to possess or disclose means native to its own constitution, substance or natural instrumentation for making the far near and annulling distance, cognising what is now beyond the body's cognisance, acting where action is now out of its reach or its domain, developing subtleties and plasticities which could not be permitted under present conditions to the needed fixity of a material frame. These and other numerous potentialities might appear and the body becomes an instrument immeasurably superior to what we can now imagine as possible. There could be an evolution from a first apprehending truth-consciousness to the utmost heights of the ascending ranges of supermind and it may pass the borders of the supermind proper itself where it begins to shadow out, develop, delineate expressive forms of life touched by a supreme pure existence, consciousness and bliss which constitute the worlds of a highest truth of existence, dynamism of *tapas*, glory and sweetness of bliss, the absolute essence and pitch of the all-creating *Ananda*. The transformation of the physical being might follow this incessant line of progression and the divine body reflect or reproduce here in a divine life on the earth something of this highest greatness and glory of the self-manifesting Spirit.

SUPERMIND AND THE LIFE DIVINE

A divine life upon earth, the ideal we have placed before us, can only come about by a spiritual change of our being and a radical and fundamental change, an evolution or revolution of our nature. The embodied being upon earth would have to rise out of the domination over it of its veils of mind, life and body into the full consciousness and possession of its spiritual reality, and its nature also would have to be lifted out of the consciousness and power of consciousness proper to a mental, vital and physical being into the greater consciousness and greater power of being and the larger and freer life of the spirit. It would not lose these former veils but they would no longer be veils or imperfect expressions but true manifestations; they would be changed into states of light, powers of spiritual life, vehicles of a spiritual existence. But this again could not be if mind, life and body were not taken up and transformed by a state of being and a force of being superior to them, a power of Supermind as much above our incomplete mental nature as that is above the nature of animal life and animated Matter, as it is immeasurably above the mere material nature.

The Supermind is in its very essence a truth-consciousness, a consciousness always free from the Ignorance which is the foundation of our present natural or evolutionary existence and from which nature in us is trying to arrive at self-knowledge and world-knowledge and a right consciousness and the right use of our existence in the universe. The Supermind, because it is a truth-consciousness, has this knowledge inherent in it and this power of true existence; its course is straight and can go direct to its aim, its field is wide and can even be made illimitable. This is because its very nature is knowledge: it has not to acquire knowledge but possesses it in its own right; its steps are not from nescience or ignorance into some imperfect light, but from truth to greater truth, from right perception to deeper perception, from intuition to intuition, from illumination to utter and boundless luminousness, from growing widenesses to the utter vasts and to very infinitude. On its summits it possesses the divine omniscience and omnipotence, but even in an evolutionary movement of its own graded self-manifestation by which it would eventually reveal its own highest heights, it must be in its very nature essentially free from ignorance and error: it starts from truth and light and moves always in truth and light. As its knowledge is always true, so too its will is always true; it does not fumble in its handling of things or stumble in its paces. In the Supermind feeling and emotion do not depart from their truth, make no slips or mistakes, do not swerve from the right and the real, cannot misuse beauty and delight or twist away from a divine rectitude. In the Supermind sense cannot mislead or deviate into the grossnesses which are here its natural imperfections and the cause of reproach, distrust and misuse by our ignorance. Even an incomplete statement made by the Supermind is a truth leading to a further truth, its incomplete action a step towards completeness. All the life and action and leading of the Supermind is guarded in its very nature from the falsehoods and uncertainties that are our lot; it moves in safety towards its perfection. Once the truth-consciousness was established here on its own sure foundation, the evolution of divine life would be a progress in felicity, a march through light to *Ananda*.

Supermind is an eternal reality of the divine Being and the divine Nature. In its own plane it already and always exists and possesses its own essential law of being; it has not to be created or to emerge or evolve into existence out of involution in Matter or out of non-existence, as it might seem to the view of mind which itself seems to its own view to have so emerged from life and Matter or to have evolved out of an involution in life and Matter. The nature of Supermind is always the same, a being of knowledge, proceeding from truth to truth, creating or rather manifesting what has to be manifested by the power of a pre-existent knowledge, not by hazard but by a self-existent destiny in the being itself, a necessity of the thing in itself and therefore inevitable. Its manifestation of the divine life will also be inevitable; its own life on its own plane is divine and, if Supermind descends upon the earth, it will bring necessarily the divine life with it and establish it here.

Supermind is the grade of existence beyond mind, life and Matter and, as mind, life and Matter have manifested on the earth, so too must Supermind in the inevitable course of things manifest in this world of Matter. In fact, a supermind is already here but it is involved, concealed behind this manifest mind, life and Matter and not yet acting overtly or in its own power: if it acts, it is through these inferior powers and modified by their characters and so not yet recognisable. It is only by the approach and arrival of the descending Supermind that it can be liberated upon earth and reveal itself in the action of our material, vital and mental parts so that these lower powers can become portions of a total divinised activity of our whole being: it is that that will bring to us a completely realised divinity or the divine life. It is indeed so that life and mind involved in Matter have realised themselves here; for only what is involved can evolve, otherwise there could be no emergence.

The manifestation of a supramental truth-consciousness is therefore the capital reality that will make the divine life possible. It is when all the movements of thought, impulse and action are governed and directed by a self-existent and luminously automatic truth-consciousness and our whole nature comes to be constituted by it and made of its stuff that the life divine will be complete and absolute. Even as it is, in reality though not in the appearance of things, it is a secret self-existent knowledge and truth that is working to manifest itself in the creation here. The Divine is already there immanent within us, ourselves are that in our inmost reality and it is this reality that we have to manifest; it is that which constitutes the urge towards the divine living and makes necessary the creation of the life divine even in this material existence.

A manifestation of the Supermind and its truth-conscious-ness is then inevitable; it must happen in this world sooner or later. But it has two aspects, a descent from above, an ascent from below, a self-revelation of the Spirit, an evolution in Nature. The ascent is necessarily an effort, a working of Nature, an urge or nisus on her side to raise her lower parts by an evolutionary or revolutionary change, conversion or transformation into the divine reality and it may happen by a process and progress or by a rapid miracle. The descent or self-revelation of the Spirit is an act of the supreme Reality from above which makes the realisation possible and it can appear either as the divine aid which brings about the fulfillment of the progress and process or as the sanction of the miracle. Evolution, as we see it in this world, is a slow and difficult process and, indeed, needs usually ages to reach abiding results; but this is because it is in its nature an emergence from inconscient beginnings, a start from nescience and a working in the ignorance of natural beings by what seems to be an unconscious force. There can be, on the contrary, an evolution in the light and no longer in the darkness, in which the evolving being is a conscious participant and cooperator, and this is precisely what must take place here. Even in the effort and progress from the Ignorance to Knowledge this must be in part if not wholly the endeavour to be made on the heights of the nature, and it must be wholly that in the final movement towards the spiritual change, realisation, transformation. It must be still more so when there is a transition across the dividing line between the Ignorance and the Knowledge and the evolution is from knowledge to greater knowledge, from consciousness to greater consciousness, from being to greater being. There is then no longer any necessity for the slow pace of the ordinary evolution; there can be rapid conversion, quick transformation after transformation, what would seem to our normal present mind a succession of miracles. An evolution on the supramental levels could well be of that nature; it could be equally, if the being so chose, a more leisurely passage of one supramental state or condition of things to something beyond but still supramental, from level to divine level, a building up of divine gradations, a free growth to the supreme Supermind or beyond it to yet undreamed levels of being, consciousness and *Ananda*.

The supramental knowledge, the truth-consciousness of the Supermind is in itself one and total: even when there is a voluntary limitation of the knowledge or what might seem to be a partial manifestation, it is so voluntarily; the limitation does not proceed from or result in any kind of ignorance, it is not a denial or withholding of knowledge, for all the rest of the truth that is not brought into expression is implicit there. Above all, there are no contradictions: whatever would seem to be opposites to the mind, here carry in themselves their own right relation and reconciling agreement, - if indeed any reconciliation were needed, for the harmony of these apparent opposites is complete. The mind tends to put the personal and the impersonal in face of each other as if they were two contraries, but the Supermind sees and realises them as, at the lowest, complements and mutually fulfilling powers of the single Reality and, more characteristically, as interfused and inseparable and themselves that single Reality. The Person has his aspect of impersonality inseparable from himself without which he could not be what he is or could not be his whole self: the Impersonal is in its truth not a state of existence, a state of consciousness and a state of bliss, but a Being self-existent, conscious of self, full of his own self-existent bliss, bliss the very substance of his being, - so, the one single and illimitable Person, Purusha. In the Supermind the finite does not cut up or limit the infinite, does not feel itself contrary to the infinite; but rather it feels its own infinity: the relative and temporal is not a contradiction of eternity but a right relation of its aspects, a native working or an imperishable feature of the eternal. Time there is only the eternal in extension and the eternal can be felt in the momentary. Thus the integral Divine is there in the Supermind and no theory of illusion or self-contradictory Maya need be thrust in to justify its way of existence. It will be obvious that an escape from life is not necessary for the Divine to find itself or its reality; it possesses that always whether in cosmic life or in its transcendent existence. The divine life cannot be a contradiction of the Divine or of the supreme reality; it is part of that reality, an aspect or expression of it and it can be nothing else. In life on the supramental plane all the Divine is possessed, and when the Supermind descends on earth, it must bring the Divine with it and make that full possession possible here.

The divine life will give to those who enter into it and possess it an increasing and finally a complete possession of the truth-consciousness and all that it carries in it; it will bring with it the realisation of the Divine in self and the Divine in Nature. All that is sought by the God-seeker will be fulfilled in his spirit and in his life as he moves towards spiritual perfection. He will become aware of the transcendent reality, possess in the self-experience the supreme existence, consciousness, bliss, be one with *Sachchidananda*. He will become one with cosmic being and universal Nature: he will contain the world in himself, in his own cosmic consciousness and feel himself one with all beings; he will see himself in all

and all in himself, become united and identified with the
Self which has become all existences. He will perceive the
beauty of the All-Beautiful and the miracle of the All-
Wonderful; he will enter in the end into the bliss of the
Brahman and live abidingly in it and for all this he will not
need to shun existence or plunge into the annihilation of
the spiritual Person in some self-extinguishing Nirvana. As
in the Self, so in Nature, he can realise the Divine. The nature
of the Divine is Light and Power and Bliss; he can feel the
divine Light and Power and Bliss above him and descending
into him, filling every strand of his nature, every cell and
atom of his being, flooding his soul and mind and life and
body, surrounding him like an illimitable sea and filling the
world, suffusing all his feeling and sense and experience,
making all his life truly and utterly divine. This and all else
that the spiritual consciousness can bring to him the divine
life will give him when it reaches its utmost completeness
and perfection and the supramental truth-consciousness is
fulfilled in all himself; but even before that he can attain to
something of it all, grow in it, live in it, once the Supermind
has descended upon him and has the direction of his
existence. All relations with the Divine will be his: the trinity
of God-knowledge, divine works and devotion to God will
open within him and move towards an utter self-giving and
surrender of his whole being and nature. He will live in God
and with God, possess God, as it is said, even plunge in him
forgetting all separate personality, but not losing it in self-
extinction. The love of God and all the sweetness of love will
remain his, the bliss of contact as well as the bliss of oneness
and the bliss of difference in oneness. All the infinite ranges
of experience of the Infinite will be his and all the joy of the
finite in the embrace of the Infinite.

The descent of the Supermind will bring to one who
receives it and is fulfilled in the truth-consciousness all the
possibilities of the divine life. It will take up not only the
whole characteristic experience which we recognise already
as constituting the spiritual life, but also all which we now
exclude from that category but which is capable of
divinisation, not excluding whatever of the earth-nature and
the earth-life can be transformed by the touch of the
Supermind and taken up into the manifested life of the Spirit.
For a divine life on earth need not be a thing apart and
exclusive having nothing to do with the common earthly

existence: it will take up human being and human life, transform what can be transformed, spiritualise whatever can be spiritualised, cast its influence on the rest and effectuate either a radical or an uplifting change, bring about a deeper communion between the universal and the individual, invade the ideal with the spiritual truth of which it is a luminous shadow and help to uplift into or towards a greater and higher existence. Mind it will uplift towards a diviner light of thought and will, life towards deeper and truer emotion and action, towards a larger power of itself, towards high aims and motives. Whatever cannot yet be raised into its own full truth of being, it will bring nearer to that fullness; whatever is not ready even for that change, will still see the possibility open to it whenever its still incomplete evolution has made it ready for self-fulfillment. Even the body, if it can bear the touch of Supermind, will become more aware of its own truth, - for there is a body consciousness that has its own instinctive truth and power of right condition and action, even a kind of unexpressed occult knowledge in the constitution of its cells and tissues which may one day become conscious and contribute to the transformation of the physical being. An awakening must come in the earth-nature and in the earth-consciousness which will be, if not the actual beginning, at least the effective preparation and the first steps of its evolution towards a new and diviner world order.

This would be the fulfillment of the divine life which the descent of Supermind and the working of the truth-consciousness taking hold of the whole nature of the living being would bring about in all who could open themselves to its power or influence. Even its first immediate effect would be on all who are capable the possibility of entering into the truth-consciousness and changing all the movements of the nature more and more into the movements of the supramental truth, truth of thought, truth of will, truth in the feelings, truth in the acts, true conditions of the whole being even to the body, eventually transformation, a divinising change. For those who could so open themselves and remain open, there would be no limitation to this development and even no fundamental difficulty; for all difficulties would be dissolved by the pressure of the supramental light and power from above pouring itself into the mind and the life-force and the body. But the result of the supramental descent need not be limited to those who could thus open themselves entirely and it need not be limited to the supramental change; there could also be a minor or secondary transformation of the mental being within a freed and perfected scope of the mental nature. In place of the human mind as it now is, a mind limited, imperfect, open at every moment to all kinds of deviation from the truth or missing of the truth, all kinds of error and openness even to the persuasions of a complete falsehood and perversion of the nature, a mind blinded and pulled down towards inconscience and ignorance, hardly arriving at knowledge, an intellect prone to interpret the higher knowledge in abstractions and indirect figures seizing and holding even the messages of the higher intuition with an uncertain and disputed grasp, there could emerge a true mind liberated and capable of the free and utmost perfection of itself and its instruments, a life governed by the free and illumined mind, a body responsive to the light and able to carry out all that the free mind and will could demand of it. This change might happen not only in the few, but extend and generalise itself in the race. This possibility, if fulfilled, would mean that the human dream of perfection, perfection of itself, of its purified and enlightened nature, of all its ways of action and living, would be no longer a dream but a truth that could be made real and humanity lifted out of the hold on it of inconscience and ignorance. The life of the mental being could be harmonised with the life of the Supermind which will then be the highest order above it, and become even an extension and annexe of the truth-consciousness, a part and province of the divine life. It is obvious that if the Supermind is there and an order of supramental being is established as the leading principle in earth-nature, as mind is now the leading principle, but with a sureness, a complete government of the earthly existence, a capacity of transformation of all upon their level and within their natural boundaries of which the mind in its imperfection was not capable, an immense change of human life, even if it did not extend to transformation, would be inevitable.

It remains to consider what might be the obstacles in the way of this possibility, especially those offered by the nature of the earth-order and its function as a field of a graded evolution in which our humanity is a stage and, it might be argued, its very imperfection an evolutionary necessity, how far could or would Supermind by its presence and government of things overcome this difficulty while respecting the principle of gradation, and whether it could not rectify the wrong and ignorant order imposed by the Ignorance and Inconscience and substitute for it a right gradation in which the perfection and divinisation would be possible. Certainly, the way for the individual would be open; whatever group of human beings aspire as united in an endeavour at a perfect individual and collective living or aspire to the divine life, would be assisted towards the attainment of its aspiration: that at least the Supermind would make its minimum consequence. But the greater possibility is also there and might even be offered to the whole of humanity. This, then, we have to consider, what would the descent of the Supermind mean for mankind and what would be its result or its promise for the whole life and evolutionary future and destiny of the human race?

SUPERMIND AND HUMANITY

What then would be the consequence for humanity of the descent of Supermind into our earthly existence, its consequence for this race born into a world of ignorance and inconscience but capable of an upward evolution of its consciousness and an ascent into the light and power and bliss of a spiritual being and spiritual nature? The descent into the earth-life of so supreme a creative power as the Supermind and its truth-consciousness could not be merely a new feature or factor added to that life or put in its front but without any other importance or only a restricted importance carrying with it no results profoundly affecting the rest of earth-nature. Especially it could not fail to exercise an immense influence on mankind as a whole, even a radical change in the aspect and prospect of its existence here, even if this power had no other capital result on the material world in which it had come down to intervene. One cannot but conclude that the influence, the change made would be far-reaching, even enormous: it would not only establish the Supermind and a supramental race of beings upon the earth, it could bring about an uplifting and transforming change in mind itself and, as an inevitable consequence, in the consciousness of man, the mental being, and would equally bring about a radical and transforming change in the principles and forms of his living, his ways of action and the whole build and tenor of his life. It would certainly open to man the access to the supramental consciousness and the supramental life; for we must suppose that it is by such a transformation that a race of supramental beings would be created, even as the human race itself has arisen by a less radical but still a considerable uplifting and enlargement of consciousness and conversion of the body's instrumentation and its indwelling and evolving mental and spiritual capacities and powers out of a first animal state. But even without any such complete transformation, the truth-principle might so far replace the principle we see here of an original ignorance seeking for knowledge and arriving only at a partial knowledge that the human mind could become a power of light, of knowledge finding itself, not the denizen of a half-way twilight or a servant and helper of the ignorance, a purveyor of mingled truth and error. Mind might even become in man, what it is in its fundamental origin, a subordinate, limited and special action of the Supermind, a sufficiently luminous receptacle of truth, and at least all falsity in its works might cease.

It could at once be objected that this would alter the whole evolutionary order and its balance and leave an incurable gap in its completeness: there would be an unbridged gulf between man and the animal and no way for the evolutionary nisus to journey over it in the progress of the consciousness from animality to divinity; for some kind of divinity would be involved in the suggested metamorphosis. It might be contended that the true process of evolution is to add a new principle, degree or stage to the already existing order and not to make any alteration in any previously established feature. Man came into being but the animal remained the animal and made no progress towards a half-humanity: all slight modifications of consciousness, capacities or habits in domestic animals produced by the association with man or by his training of them are only slight alterations of the animal intelligence. Still less can the plant move towards animal consciousness or brute Matter become in the slightest degree, even subconsciously or half subconsciously, aware of itself or responsive or reactive. The fundamental distinctions remain and must remain unaltered in the cosmic order. But this objection presumes that the new humanity must be all of one level; there may well be gradations of consciousness in it which would bridge the distance between its least developed elements and the higher animals who, although they cannot pass into a semi-human kind, might still progress towards a higher animal intelligence: for certain experiments show that these are not all entirely unprogressive. These gradations would serve the purpose of the transition quite as well as the least developed humans in the present scale without leaving a gap so wide as to disturb the evolutionary order of the universe. A considerable saltus can, as it is, be observed separating the different orders, Matter and the plant, the plant and the lower animals, one species of animals and another, as well as that always existing and large enough between the highest animal and man. There would therefore be no incurable breach in the evolutionary order, no such distance between human mind and animal mind, between the new type of human being and the old animal level as could not be overleaped or would create an unbridgeable gulf for the most developed animal soul in its passage to the least developed type of the new humanity. A leap, a saltus, there would be, as there is now; but it would not be between animality and divinity, from animal mind to Supermind: it would be between a most highly developed animal mind turning towards human possibilities - for without that the passage from animal to man could not be achieved - and a human mind waking to the possibility, not yet the full achievement, of its own higher yet unattained capacities.

One result of the intervention of Supermind in the earth-nature, the descent of the supreme creative Truth-Power, might well be a change in the law of evolution, its method and its arrangement: a larger element of the principle of evolution through knowledge might enter into the forces of the material universe.

This might extend itself from a first beginning in the new creation and produce increasing effects in the order which is now wholly an evolution in the ignorance, and indeed starts from the complete nescience of the Inconscient and proceeds towards what can be regarded even in its highest attainment of knowledge as a lesser ignorance, since it is more a representation than a direct and complete possession of knowledge. If man began to develop the powers and means of a higher knowledge in something like fullness, if the developing animal opened the door of his mentality to beginnings of conscious thought and even a rudimentary reason, - at his highest he is not so irrevocably far from that even now, - if the plant developed its first subconscient reactions and attained to some kind of primary nervous sensitiveness, if Matter, which is a blind form of the Spirit, were to become more alive with the hidden power within it and to offer more readily the secret sense of things, the occult realities it covers, as for instance, the record of the past it always preserves even in its dumb inconscience or the working of its involved forces and invisible movements revealing veiled powers in material nature to a subtler generalised perception of the new human intelligence, this would be an immense change promising greater changes in the future, but it would mean only an uplifting and not a disturbance of the universal order.

Evolution would itself evolve, but it would not be perturbed or founder.

It is difficult for us to conceive in theory or admit as a practical possibility the transformation of the human mentality I have suggested as a change that would naturally take place under the lead of the supramental Truth-consciousness, because our notions about mind are rooted in an experience of human mentality in a world which starts from inconscience and proceeds through a first almost complete nescience and a slowly lessening ignorance towards a high degree but always incomplete scope and imperfect method of only partially equipped knowledge which does not serve fully the needs of a consciousness always pushing towards its own still immeasurably distant absolute. The visible imperfections and limitations of mind in the present stage of its evolution here we take as part of its very nature; but in fact the boundaries in which it is still penned are only temporary limits and measures of its still incomplete evolutionary advance; its defects of methods and means are faults of its immaturity and not proper to the constitution of its being; its achievement, although extraordinary under the hampering conditions of the mental being weighed down by its instrumentation in an earthly body, is far below and not beyond what will be possible to it in its illumined future. For mind is not in its very nature an inventor of errors, a father of lies bound down to a capacity of falsehood, wedded to its own mistakes and the leader of a stumbling life as it too largely is at present owing to our human shortcomings: it is in its origin a principle of light, an instrument put forth from the Supermind and, though set to work within limits and even set to create limits, yet the limits are luminous borders for a special working, voluntary and purposive bounds, a surface of the finite ever extending itself under the eye of infinity. It is this character of Mind that will reveal itself under the touch of Supermind and make human mentality an adjunct and a minor instrumentation of the supramental knowledge. It will even be possible for the mind no longer limited by the intellect to become capable of a sort of mental gnosis, a luminous reproduction of the Truth in a diminished working, extending the power of the Light not only to its own but to lower levels of consciousness in their climb towards self-transcendence. Overmind, Intuition, Illumined Mind and what I have called Higher Mind, these and other levels of a spiritualised and liberated mentality, will be able to reflect in the uplifted human mind and its purified and exalted feeling and force of life and action something of their powers and prepare the ascent of the soul to their own plateaus and peaks of an ascending existence.

This is essentially the change which can be contemplated as a result of the new evolutionary order, and it would mean a considerable extension of the evolutionary field itself and will answer the question as to the result on humanity of the advent of Supermind into the earth-nature.

If mind in its origin from Supermind is itself a power of Supermind, a principle of Light and a power of Light or a force for Knowledge specialised in its action for a subordinate purpose, yet it assumes a different aspect when in the working out of this purpose it separates itself more and more from the supramental light, from the immediate power and supporting illumination of the supramental principle. It is as it departs more and more in this direction from its own highest truth that it becomes a creator or parent of ignorance and is or seems to be the highest power in a world of ignorance; it becomes itself subject to ignorance and seems only to arrive at a partial and imperfect knowledge. The reason of this decline is that it is used by the Supermind principally for the work of differentiation which is necessary if there is to be a creation and a universe. In the Supermind itself, in all its creation there is this differentiating power, the manifestation of the One in the Many and the Many in the One; but the One is never forgotten or lost in its multiplicity which always consciously depends upon and never takes precedence over the eternal oneness. In the mind, on the contrary, the differentiation, the multiplicity does take precedence and the conscious sense of the universal oneness is lost and the separated unit seems to exist for itself and by itself as a sufficient self-conscious integer or in inanimate objects as the inconscient integer.

It should be noted, however, that a world or plane of mind need not be a reign of ignorance where falsity, error or nescience must have a place; it may be only a voluntary self-limitation of knowledge. It could be a world where all possibilities capable of being determined by mind could manifest themselves in the successions of Time and find a true form and field of their action, the expressive figure of themselves, their capacity of self-development, self-realisation of a kind, self-discovery. This is actually what we meet when we follow in psychic experience the line of descent by which the involution takes place which ends in Matter and the creation of the material universe. What we see here is not the planes or worlds of the descent in which mind and life can keep something of their truth and something of the light of the spirit, something of their true and real being; here we see an original inconscience and a struggle of life and mind and spirit to evolve out of the material inconscience and in a resultant ignorance to find themselves and grow towards their full capacity and highest existence. If mind succeeds in that endeavour there is no reason why it should not recover its true character and be once more a principle and power of Light and even in its own way aid in the workings of a true and complete knowledge. At its highest it might pass out of its limitations into the supramental truth and become part and function of the supramental knowledge or at the least serve for a minor work of differentiation in the consensus of that knowledge: in the lower degree below Supermind it might be a mental gnosis, a spiritual or spiritualised perception, feeling, activity, sense which could do the works of knowledge and not of ignorance. Even at a still lower level it could be an increasingly luminous passage leading from light to light, from truth to truth and no longer a circling in the mazes of half-truth and half-nescience. This would not be possible in a world where untransformed mind or human mind burdened with its hampering disabilities, as it now is, will still be the leader or the evolution's highest achievement, but with Supermind for the leading and dominant power this might well happen, and might even be regarded as one result and an almost inevitable result of its descent into the human world and its touch on the mind of humanity.

How far this would go, whether the whole of humanity would be touched or only a part of it ready for the change, would depend on what was intended or possible in the continued order of the universe. If the old evolutionary principle and order must be preserved, then only a section of the race would pass onward, the rest would keep the old human position, level and function in the ascending order.

But even so there must be a passage or bridge between the two levels or orders of being by which the evolution would make its transition from one to the other; the mind would there be capable of contact with and modification by the supramental truth and thus would be the means of the soul's passing on upward: there must be a status of mind capable of receiving and growing in the Light towards Supermind though not reaching it; through that, as even now happens in a lesser degree through a dimmer medium, the lustre of a greater truth would send down its rays for the liberation and uplift of the soul in the ignorance. Supermind is here veiled behind a curtain and, though not organised for its own characteristic action, it is the true cause of all creation here, the power for the growth of truth and knowledge and the ascension of the soul towards the hidden Reality. But in a world where Supermind has made its appearance, it could hardly be a separate factor isolated from the rest, it would inevitably not only create superman but change and uplift man. A total change of the mental principle, such as has been suggested, cannot be ruled out as impossible.

Mind as we know it, as a power of consciousness quite distinct from Supermind, no longer a power devolved from it, connected with it and dependent upon it, but practically divorced from its luminous origin, is marked by several characteristics which we conceive to be the very signs of its nature: but some of these belong to Supermind also and the difference is in the way and scope of their action, not in their stuff or in their principle. The difference is that mind is not a power of whole knowledge and only when it begins to pass beyond itself a power of direct knowledge: it receives rays of the truth but does not live in the sun; it sees as through glasses and its knowledge is coloured by its instruments, it cannot see with the naked eye or look straight at the sun. It is not possible for mind to take its stand in the solar centre or anywhere in the radiant body or even on the shining circumference of the orb of perfect truth and acquire or share in its privilege of infallible or absolute knowledge. It would be only if it had already drawn near to the light of Supermind that it could live anywhere near this sun in the full splendour of its rays, in something of the full and direct blaze of Truth, and the human mind even at its highest is far from that; it can only live at most in a limited circle, in some narrow beginnings of a pure insight, a direct vision and it would take long for it, even in surpassing itself, to reach to an imitative and fragmentary reflection of a dream of the limited omniscience and omnipotence which is the privilege of a delegated divinity, of the god, of a demiurge. It is a power for creation, but either tentative and uncertain and succeeding by good chance or the favour of circumstance or else, if assured by some force of practical ability or genius, subject to flaw or pent within unescapable limits. Its highest knowledge is often abstract, lacking in a concrete grasp; it has to use expedients and unsure means of arrival, to rely upon reasoning, argumentation and debate, inferences, divinations, set methods of inductive or deductive logic, succeeding only if it is given correct and complete data and even then liable to reach on the same data different results and varying consequences; it has to use means and accept results of a method which is hazardous even when making a claim to certitude and of which there would be no need if it had a direct or a supra-intellectual knowledge. It is not necessary to push the description further; all this is the very nature of our terrestrial ignorance and its shadow hangs on even to the thought and vision of the sage and the seer and can be escaped only if the principle of a truth-conscious supramental knowledge descends and takes up the governance of the earth-nature.

It should be noted, however, that even at the bottom of the involutionary descent, in the blind eclipse of consciousness in Matter, in the very field of the working of the Inconscient there are signs of the labour of an infallible force, the drive of a secret consciousness and its promptings, as if the Inconscient itself were secretly informed or impelled by a Power with a direct and absolute knowledge; its acts of creation are infinitely surer than the workings of our human consciousness at its best or the normal workings of the Life-power. Matter, or rather the Energy in Matter seems to have a more certain knowledge, a more infallible operation of its own and its mechanism once set going can be trusted for the most part to do its work accurately and well. It is so that man is able, taking hold of a material energy, to mechanise it for his own ends and trust it under proper conditions to do for him his work. The self-creating life-power, amazingly abundant in its invention and fantasy, yet seems to be more capable of flaw, aberration and failure; it is as if its greater consciousness carried in it a greater capacity for error. Yet it is sure enough ordinarily in its workings: but as consciousness increases in the forms and operations of life, and most when mind enters in, disturbances also increase as if the increase of consciousness brought with it not only richer possibilities but more possibilities of stumbling, error, flaw and failure. In mind, in man, we seem to reach the height of this antinomy, the greatest, highest, widest reach and achievements of consciousness, the greatest amount of uncertainty, defect, failure and error. This, we may conjecture, may be because in inconscient Nature there is a truth of energy at work which follows infallibly its own law, an energy which can walk blindfold without stumbling because the automatic law of the truth is within it, operating surely without swerving or mistake when there is no external intervention or interference. But in all normally automatic processes of existence there is this law: even the body has an unexpressed knowledge of its own, a just instinct in its action within certain limits and this when not interfered with by life's desires and mind's errors can work with a certain accuracy and sureness. But Supermind alone has the truth-consciousness in full and, if this comes down and intervenes, mind, life and body too can attain to the full power of the truth in them and their full possibility of perfection. This, no doubt, would not take place at once, but an evolutionary progress towards it could begin and grow with increasing rapidity towards its fullness. All men might not reach that fullness till a later time, but still the human mind could come to stand perfected in the Light and a new humanity take its place as part of the new order.

This is the possibility we have to examine. If it is destined to fulfill itself, if man is not doomed to remain always as a vassal of the Ignorance, the disabilities of the human mind on which we have dwelt are not such as must remain irredeemably in possession and binding for ever. It could develop higher means and instrumentalities, pass over the last borders of the Ignorance into a higher knowledge, grow too strong to be held back by the animal nature. There would be a liberated mind escaping from ignorance into light, aware of its affiliation to Supermind, a natural agent of Supermind and capable of bringing down the supramental influence into the lower reaches of being, a creator in the light, a discoverer in the depths, an illuminant in the darkness, helping perhaps to penetrate even the Inconscient with the rays of a secret Superconscience. There would be a new mental being not only capable of standing enlightened in the radiance of the Supermind but able to climb consciously towards it and into it, training life and body to reflect and hold something of the supramental light, power and bliss, aspiring to release the secret divinity into self-finding and self-fulfillment and self-poise, aspiring towards the ascension to the divine consciousness, able to receive and bear the descent of the divine light and power, fitting itself to be a vessel of the divine Life.

SUPERMIND IN EVOLUTION

A new humanity would then be a race of mental beings on the earth and in the earthly body, but delivered from its present conditions in the reign of the cosmic Ignorance so far as to be possessed of a perfected mind, a mind of light which could even be a subordinate action of the supermind or Truth-Consciousness, and in any case capable of the full possibilities of mind acting as a recipient of that truth and at least a secondary action of it in thought and life. It could even be a part of what could be described as a divine life upon earth and at least the beginnings of an evolution in the Knowledge and no longer entirely or predominantly in the Ignorance. How far this would go, whether it would eventually embrace the whole of humanity or only an advanced portion of it, would depend upon the intention in the evolution itself, on the intention in whatever cosmic or transcendent Will is guiding the movements of the universe.

We have supposed not only the descent of the supermind upon the earth but its embodiment in a supramental race with all its natural consequences and a new total action in which the new humanity would find its complete development and its assured place in the new order. But it is clear that all this could only come as a result of the evolution which is already taking place upon earth extending far beyond its present bounds and passing into a radically new movement governed by a new principle in which mind and man would be subordinate elements and no longer mind the utmost achievement or man the head or leader. The evolution we see around us at present is not of that kind and, it might be said, shows few signs of such a possibility, so few that the reason, at present our only sure guide, has no right to hazard belief in it. Earth, the earth we see, with its life deeply immersed and founded in inconscience and ignorance, is not built for such a development or capable of holding such an advent; its materiality and limitations condemn it to be permanently the field of a far inferior order. It may be said too that for such an order there must be a place somewhere and even if supermind is not a mere unwarranted speculation and is a concrete reality, there is no need and no place for its embodying itself here. Mind, as marking the full play of the knowledge possible to the ignorance, must have its field somewhere and to keep the earth as its natural field would best serve the economy of cosmic Nature. A materialistic philosophy would admit of no possibility of a divine life in Matter; but even a philosophy admitting a soul or spirit or a spiritual terminus of the evolutionary movement here could very well deny the capacity of earth for a divine life: a divine existence could only be achieved by a departure from earth and the body. Even if cosmic existence is not an illusion or Maya, a divine or a completely spiritual being is likely to be possible only in another less material world or only in the pure spirit. At any rate, to the normal human reason the odds seem to be heavily against any early materialisation on earth of anything divine.

Again, if too strong a stress is laid on the present or apparent character of the evolution here as it is presented to us by physical science, it might be urged that there is no warrant for expecting any emergence of a principle higher than human mind or of any such thing as superhuman beings in a world of Matter.

Consciousness is itself dependent upon Matter and material agencies for its birth and its operations and an infallible Truth-consciousness, such as we suppose supermind to be, would be a contradiction of these conditions and must be dismissed as a chimera. Fundamentally, physical science regards evolution as a development of forms and vital activities; the development of a larger and more capable consciousness is a subordinate result of the development of life and form and not a major or essential characteristic or circumstance and it cannot go beyond limits determined by the material origin of mind and life. Mind has shown itself capable of many extraordinary achievements, but independence of the material organ or of physical conditions or a capability for any such thing as a power of direct and absolute knowledge not acquired by material means would be beyond the conditions imposed by Nature. At a certain point therefore the evolution of consciousness can go no further. Even if a something definite and independent which we call a soul exists, it is limited by its natural conditions here where Matter is the basis, physical life the condition, mind the highest possible instrument; there is no possibility of an action of consciousness apart from the body or surpassing this physical, vital or mental Nature. This fixes the limits of our evolution here.

It might be suggested also that until something clearly recognisable like supermind manifests itself with some definiteness and fullness or until it descends and takes possession of our earth-consciousness, we cannot be certain that it exists; till then mind holds the place as a general arbiter or field of reference for all knowledge and mind is incapable of any certain or absolute knowledge; it has to doubt all, to test all and yet to achieve all, but cannot be secure in its knowledge or its achievement. That, incidentally, establishes the necessity of such a principle as the supermind or Truth-consciousness in any intelligible universe, for without it there is no issue, no goal for either life or knowledge. Consciousness cannot achieve its own entire meaning, its own supreme result without it; it will end in an inconsequence or a fiasco. To become aware of its own truth and all truth is the very aim of its existence and it cannot do so, so long as it has to tend towards truth, towards knowledge in ignorance and through the ignorance: it must develop or it must reach a power of itself whose very nature is to know, to see, to possess in its own power. This is what we call supermind and, once it is admitted, all the rest becomes intelligible. But till then we are in doubt and it may be contended that even if supermind is admitted as a reality, there can be no certainty of its advent and reign: till then all effort towards it may end in failure. It is not enough that the supermind should be actually there above us, its descent a possibility or a future intention in Nature. We have no certainty of the reality of this descent until it becomes an objectivised fact in our earthly being. Light has often tried to descend upon the earth, but the Light remains unfulfilled and incomplete; man may reject the Light, the world is still full of darkness and the advent seems to be little more than a chance; this doubt is to some extent justified by the actualities of the past and still existing possibilities of the future. Its power to stand would disappear only if supermind is once admitted as a consequent part of the order of the universe. If the evolution tends from Matter to

Supermind, it must also tend to bring down Supermind into Matter and the consequences are inevitable.

The whole trouble of this incertitude arises from the fact that we do not look straight at the whole truth of the world as it is and draw from it the right conclusion as to what the world must be and cannot fail to be. This world is, no doubt, based ostensibly upon Matter, but its summit is Spirit and the ascent towards Spirit must be the aim and justification of its existence and the pointer to its meaning and purpose. But the natural conclusion to be drawn from the supremacy and summit existence of Spirit is clouded by a false or imperfect idea of spirituality which has been constructed by intellect in its ignorance and even by its too hasty and one-sided grasp at knowledge. The Spirit has been thought of not as something all-pervading and the secret essence of our being, but as something only looking down on us from the heights and drawing us only towards the heights and away from the rest of existence. So we get the idea of our cosmic and individual being as a great illusion, and departure from it and extinction in our consciousness of both individual and cosmos as the only hope, the sole release. Or we build up the idea of the earth as a world of ignorance, suffering and trial and our only future an escape into heavens beyond; there is no divine prospect for us here, no fulfillment possible even with the utmost evolution on earth in the body, no victorious transformation, no supreme object to be worked out in terrestrial existence. But if supermind exists, if it descends, if it becomes the ruling principle, all that seems impossible to mind becomes not only possible but inevitable. If we look closely, we shall see that there is a straining of mind and life on their heights towards their own perfection, towards some divine fulfillment, towards their own absolute. That and not only something beyond and elsewhere is the true sign, the meaning of this constant evolution and the labour of continual birth and rebirth and the spiral ascent of Nature. But it is only by the descent of supermind and the fulfillment of mind and life by their self-exceeding that this secret intention in things, this hidden meaning of Spirit and Nature can become utterly overt and in its totality realisable. This is the evolutionary aspect and significance of supermind, but in truth it is an eternal principle existing covertly even in the material universe, the secret supporter of all creation, it is that which makes the emergence of consciousness possible and certain in an apparently inconscient world and compels a climb in Nature towards a supreme spiritual Reality. It is, in fact, an already and always existent plane of being, the nexus of Spirit and Matter, holding in its truth and reality and making certain the whole meaning and aim of the universe.

If we disregard our present ideas of evolution, all changes, - if we can regard consciousness and not life and form as the fundamental and essential evolutionary principle and its emergence and full development of its possibilities as the object of the evolutionary urge. The inconscience of Matter cannot be an insuperable obstacle; for in this inconscience can be detected an involved consciousness which has to evolve; life and mind are steps and instruments of that evolution; the purposeful drive and workings of the inconscient material Energy are precisely such as we can attribute to the presence of an involved consciousness, automatic, not using thought like the mind but guided by something like an inherent material instinct practically infallible in all its steps, not yet cognitive but miraculously creative. The entirely and inherently enlightened Truth-consciousness we attribute to supermind would be the same reality appearing at an ultimate stage of the evolution, finally evolved and no longer wholly involved as in Matter or partly and imperfectly evolved and therefore capable of imperfection and error as in life and mind, now possessed of its own natural fullness and perfection, luminously automatic, infallible. All the objections to a complete evolutionary possibility then fall away; it would, on the contrary, be the inevitable consequence contained not only in Nature as a whole but even in material Nature.

In this vision of things the universe will reveal itself in its unity and totality as a manifestation of a single Being, Nature as its power of manifestation, evolution as its process of gradual self-revelation here in Matter. We would see the divine series of the worlds as a ladder of ascent from Matter to supreme Spirit; there would reveal itself the possibility, the prospect of a supreme manifestation by the conscious and no longer a veiled and enigmatic descent of the Spirit and its powers in their fullness even into this lowest world of Matter. The riddle of the universe need be no longer a riddle; the dubious mystery of things would put off its enigma, its constant ambiguity, the tangled writings would become legible and intelligible. In this revelation, supermind would take its natural place and no longer be a matter of doubt or questioning to an intelligence bewildered by the complexity of the world; it would appear as the inevitable consequence of the nature of mind, life and Matter, the fulfillment of their meaning, their inherent principle and tendencies, the necessary perfection of their imperfection, the summit to which all are climbing, the consummation of divine existence, consciousness and bliss to which it is leading, the last result of the birth of things and supreme goal of this progressive manifestation which we see here in life.

The full emergence of supermind may be accomplished by a sovereign manifestation, a descent into earth-consciousness and a rapid assumption of its powers and disclosing of its forms and the creation of a supramental race and a supramental life: this must indeed be the full result of its action in Nature. But this has not been the habit of evolutionary Nature in the past upon earth and it may well be that this supramental evolution also will fix its own periods, though it cannot be at all a similar development to that of which earth has hitherto been the witness. But once it has begun, all must unavoidably and perfectly manifest and all parts of Nature must tend towards a greatest possible luminousness and perfection. It is this certainty that authorises us to believe that mind and humanity also will tend towards a realisation that will be far beyond our present dreams of perfection. A mind of light will replace the present confusion and trouble of this earthly ignorance; it is likely that even those parts of humanity which cannot reach it will yet be aware of its possibility and consciously tend towards it; not only so, but the life of humanity will be enlightened, uplifted, governed, harmonised by this luminous principle and even the body become something much less powerless, obscure and animal in its propensities and capable instead of a new and harmonised perfection. It is this possibility that we have to look at and that would mean a new humanity uplifted into Light, capable of a spiritualised being and action, open to governance by some light of the Truth-consciousness, capable even on the mental level and in its own order of something that might be called the beginning of a divinised life.

MIND OF LIGHT

A new humanity means for us the appearance, the development of a type or race of mental beings whose principle of mentality would be no longer a mind in the Ignorance seeking for knowledge but even in its knowledge bound to the Ignorance, a seeker after Light but not its natural possessor, open to the Light but not an inhabitant of the Light, not yet a perfected instrument, truth-conscious and delivered out of the Ignorance. Instead, it would be possessed already of what could be called a mind of Light, a mind capable of living in the truth, capable of being truth-conscious and manifesting in its life a direct in place of an indirect knowledge. Its mentality would be an instrument of the Light and no longer of the Ignorance. At its highest it would be capable of passing into the supermind and from the new race would be recruited the race of supramental beings who would appear as the leaders of the evolution in earth-nature. Even, the highest manifestations of a mind of Light would be an instrumentality of the supermind, a part of it or a projection from it, a stepping beyond humanity into the superhumanity of the supramental principle. Above all, its possession would enable the human being to rise beyond the normalities of his present thinking, feeling and being into those highest powers of the mind in its self-exceedings which intervene between our mentality and supermind and can be regarded as steps leading towards the greater and more luminous principle. This advance like others in the evolution might not be reached and would naturally not be reached at one bound, but from the very beginning it would be inevitable: the pressure of the supermind creating from above out of itself the mind of Light would compel this certainty of the eventual outcome. The first gleamings of the new Light would carry in themselves the seed of its highest flamings; even in the first beginnings, the certainty of their topmost powers would be there; for this is the constant story of each evolutionary emergence: the principle of its highest perfection lies concealed in the involution which precedes and necessitates the evolution of the secret principle.

For throughout the story of evolution there are two complementary aspects which constitute its action and are necessary to its totality; there is hidden in the involution of Nature the secret power and principle of being which lies concealed under the veil cast on it by material Nature and there is carried in that Nature itself the inevitable force of the principle compelling the process of emergence of its inherent powers and characters, the essential features which constitute its reality. As the evolutionary principle emerges, there are also two constant features of the process of the emergence: there are the gradations by which it climbs out of the involution and manifests more and more of its power, its possibilities, the force of the Godhead within it, and there is a constant manifestation of all types and forms of its being which are the visible, indicative and efficient embodiments of its essential nature. There appear in the evolutionary process organised forms and activities of Matter, the types of life and the living beings, the types of mind and the thinking beings, the luminosities and greatnesses of the spiritual principle and the spiritual beings whose nature, character, personality, mark the stages of the ascent towards the highest heights of the evolution and the ultimate largest manifestation of what it is in itself and must become by the force of time and the all-revealing Spirit. This is the real sense and drive of what we see as evolution: the multiplication and variation of forms is only the means of its process. Each gradation contains the possibility and the certainty of the grades beyond it: the emergence of more and more developed forms and powers points to more perfected forms and greater powers beyond them, and each emergence of consciousness and the conscious beings proper to it enables the rise to a greater consciousness beyond and the greater order of beings up to the ultimate godheads of which Nature is striving and is destined to show herself capable. Matter developed its organised forms until it became capable of embodying living organisms; then life rose from the subconscience of the plant into conscious animal formations and through them to the thinking life of man.

Mind founded in life developed intellect, developed its types of knowledge and ignorance, truth and error till it reached the spiritual perception and illumination and now can see as in a glass dimly the possibility of supermind and a truth-conscious existence. In this inevitable ascent the mind of Light is a gradation, an inevitable stage. As an evolving principle it will mark a stage in the human ascent and evolve a new type of human being; this development must carry in it an ascending gradation of its own powers and types of an ascending humanity which will embody more and more the turn towards spirituality, capacity for Light, a climb towards a divinised manhood and the divine life.

In the birth of the mind of Light and its ascension into its own recognisable self and its true status and right province there must be, in the very nature of things as they are and very nature of the evolutionary process as it is at present, two stages. In the first, we can see the mind of Light gathering itself out of the Ignorance, assembling its constituent elements, building up its shapes and types, however imperfect at first, and pushing them towards perfection till it can cross the border of the Ignorance and appear in the Light, in its own Light. In the second stage we can see it developing itself in that greater natural light, taking its higher shapes and forms till it joins the supermind and lives as its subordinate portion or its delegate. In each of these stages it will define its own grades and manifest the order of its beings who will embody it and give to it a realised life.

Thus there will be built up, first, even in the Ignorance itself, the possibility of a human ascent towards a divine living; then there will be, by the illumination of this mind of Light in the greater realisation of what may be called a gnostic mentality, in a transformation of the human being, even before the supermind is reached, even in the earth-consciousness and in a humanity transformed, an illumined divine life.

SUPERMIND AND MIND OF LIGHT

The essential character of Supermind is a Truth-Consciousness which knows by its own inherent right of nature, by its own light; it has not to arrive at knowledge but possesses it. It may indeed, especially in its evolutionary action, keep knowledge behind its apparent consciousness and bring it forward as if from behind the veil; but even then this veil is only an appearance and does not really exist: the knowledge was always there, the consciousness its possessor and present revealer. This too is only in the evolutionary play and on the supramental plane itself the consciousness lives always in an immediacy of knowledge and acts by a direct immediacy of knowledge. In Mind as we see it here the action is very different; it starts from an apparent absence of knowledge, a seeming ignorance or nescience, even, in material Nature, from an inconscience in which any kind of knowing does not seem at all to exist. It reaches knowledge or the action of knowledge by steps which are not at all immediate but rather knowledge at first seems utterly impossible and foreign to the very substance of this Matter. Yet, in the blindness of Matter itself there are signs of a concealed consciousness which in its hidden fundamental being sees and has the power to act according to its vision and even by an infallible immediacy which is inherent in its nature. This is the same Truth that is apparent in Supermind but is here involved and seems not to be. The Mind of Light is a subordinate action of Supermind, dependent upon it even when not apparently springing direct from it, in which the secret of this connection becomes evident and palpable.

The Truth-Consciousness is not only a power of knowledge; it is a being of consciousness and knowledge, a luminous many-sided dynamis and play of the omniscient Spirit; in it there can be a spiritual feeling, a spiritual sensation, a spiritual essentiality of substance that knows and reveals, that acts and manifests in an omniscience which is one with omnipotence. In Mind this Truth-Consciousness and these workings of the Truth-Consciousness can be there and even though it limits itself in Mind and has a subordinate or an indirect working, its action can be essentially the same. There can even be a hidden immediacy which hints at the presence of something absolute and is evidence of the same omnipotence and omniscience. In the Mind of Light when it becomes full-orbed this character of the Truth reveals itself though in a garb that is transparent even when it seems to cover: for this too is a truth-consciousness and a self-power of knowledge. This too proceeds from the Supermind and depends upon it even though it is limited and subordinate. What we have called specifically the Mind of Light is indeed the last of a series of descending planes of consciousness in which the Supermind veils itself by a self-chosen limitation or modification of its self-manifesting activities, but its essential character remains the same: there is in it an action of light, of truth, of knowledge in which inconscience, ignorance and error claim no place. It proceeds from knowledge to knowledge; we have not yet crossed over the borders of the truth-conscious into ignorance. The methods also are those of a self-luminous knowing and seeing and feeling and a self-fulfilling action within its own borders; there is no need to seek for something missing, no fumbling, no hesitation: all is still a gnostic action of a gnostic power and principle. There has been a descent from full Supermind into Mind, but this Mind though a self-limited is not yet an agnostic consciousness unsure of itself or unsure of its workings; there is still a comprehending or an apprehending consciousness which goes straight to its object and does not miss its mark or have to hunt for it in the dark or in insufficient light: it sees, knows, puts its hand immediately on things of self and things of Nature. We have passed into Mind but Mind has still not broken its inherent connection with the supramental principle.

Still there is an increasing self-limitation which begins even with Overmind: Overmind is separated by only a luminous border on the full light and power of the supramental Truth and it still commands direct access to all that Supermind can give it. There is a further limitation or change of characteristic action at each step downwards from Overmind to Intuition, from Intuition to Illumined Mind, from Illumined Mind to what I have called the Higher Mind: the Mind of Light is a transitional passage by which we can pass from supermind and superhumanity to an illumined humanity. For the new humanity will be capable of at least a partly divinised way of seeing and living because it will live in the light and in knowledge and not in the obscuration of the Ignorance.

Still, again there will be a difference between the superhuman and the human, a difference in nature and power but a difference especially in the access and way of admission to the Truth-Consciousness and its activities: there may indeed be two orders of its truth, direct and half-direct, immediate and near or even only a reception at a distance. But this we must consider afterwards; at present it is sufficient to mark certain differences in the descending order of gnostic mind which culminates here. We may say that there is a higher hemisphere of our being in which Mind luminous and aware of its workings still lives in the Light and can be seen as a subordinate power of the Supermind; it is still an agent of the Truth-Consciousness, a gnostic power that has not descended into the mental ignorance; it is capable of a mental gnosis that preserves its connection with the superior light and acts by its power. This is the character of Overmind in its own plane and of all the powers that are dependent on the Overmind: the Supermind works there but at one remove, as if in something that it has put forth from itself but which is no longer entirely itself but is still a delegate of the Truth and invested with its authority. We are moving towards a transitional border beyond which lies the possibility of the Ignorance, but the Ignorance is not yet here. In the order of the evolutionary descent we stand in the Mind of Light on that border and a step downward can carry us beyond it into the beginnings of an ignorance which still bears on its face something of the luminosity that it is leaving behind it. On the other hand, in the ascending order of the evolution we reach a transition in which we see the light, are turned towards it, reflected in our consciousness and one further step carries us into the domain of the Light. The Truth becomes visible and audible to us and we are in immediate communication with its messages and illuminations and can grow into it and be made one with its substance. Thus there is a succession of ranges of consciousness which we can speak of as Mind but which belongs practically to the higher hemisphere although in their ontological station they are within the domain of the lower hemisphere. For the whole of being is a connected totality and there is in it no abrupt passage from the principle of Truth and Light into their opposite. The creative truth of things works and can work infallibly even in the Inconscient: the Spirit is there in Matter and it has made a series of steps by which it can travel from it to its own heights in an uninterrupted line of gradations: the depths are linked to the heights and the Law of the one Truth creates and works everywhere.

Even in the material world which seems to us a world of ignorance, a world of the workings of a blind and inconscient Force starting from inconscience and proceeding through Ignorance and reaching with difficulty towards an imperfect Light and Knowledge, there is still a secret Truth in things which arranges all, guides towards the Self many contrary powers of being and rises towards its own heights where it can manifest its own highest truth and fulfill the secret purpose of the universe. Even this material world of existence is built upon a pattern of the truth in things which we call Law of Nature, a truth from which we climb to a greater truth until we emerge in the Light of the Supreme. This world is not really created by a blind force of Nature: even in the Inconscient the presence of the supreme Truth is at work; there is a seeing Power behind it which acts infallibly and the steps of the Ignorance itself are guided even when they seem to stumble; for, what we call the Ignorance is a cloaked Knowledge, a Knowledge at work in a body not its own but moving towards its own supreme self-discovery. This Knowledge is the covert Supermind which is the support of the creation and is leading all towards itself and guides behind this multitude of minds and creatures and objects which seem each to be following its own law of nature; in this vast and apparently confused mass of existence there is a law, a one truth of being, a guiding and fulfilling purpose of the world-existence. The Supermind is veiled here and does not work according to its characteristic law of being and self-knowledge, but without it nothing could reach its aim. A world governed by an ignorant mind would soon drift into a chaos; it could not in fact come into existence or remain in existence unless supported by the secret Omniscience of which it is the cover; a world governed by a blind inconscient force might repeat constantly the same mechanical workings but it would mean nothing and arrive nowhere. This could not be the cause of an evolution that creates life out of Matter, out of life mind, and a gradation of planes of Matter, Life and Mind culminating in the emergence of Supermind. The secret truth that emerges in Supermind has been there all the time, but now it manifests itself and the truth in things and the meaning of our existence.

It is in this series of the order of existence and as the last word of the lower hemisphere of being, the first word of the higher hemisphere that we have to look at the Mind of Light and see what is its nature and the powers which characterise it and which it uses for its self-manifestation and workings, its connection with Supermind and its consequences and possibilities for the life of a new humanity.

BIBLIOGRAPHY

SRI AUROBINDO'S PRINCIPAL WORKS[1]

Sri Aurobindo's *magnum opus, The Life Divine,* is a 950-page philosophical and spiritual treatise, first published serially in the philosophical monthly *Arya* 1914-1921. The other contributions that he made to this extraordinary journal were later collected into the works that comprise virtually all of the basic insights that Sri Aurobindo had gleaned from his years of seeking up to that time. In addition to *The Life Divine,* these works include: *The Synthesis of Yoga, The Human Cycle, The Ideal of Human Unity, The Future Poetry, On the Veda (Secret of the Veda), Isha Upanishad, Kena Upanishad, Essays on the Gita,* and *The Foundations of Indian Culture.* The only major work not included in this list is *Savitri: A Legend* and *A Symbol,* Sri Aurobindo's epic poem of 23,813 lines of blank verse, which he revised constantly until his death in 1950. In addition to *The Mind of Light* (published originally and continuously in India under the title *Supramental Manifestation on Earth*), which is perhaps the best general introduction to Sri Aurobindo's system, there are several works that provide

---

[1] Unless otherwise specified, works by Sri Aurobindo and his disciples are published by Sri Aurobindo Ashram Press, Sri Aurobindo Ashram, Pondicherry, India 605002. Most of the major writings of Sri Aurobindo, the *Sri Aurobindo Selected Writings Software CD ROM,* as well as a number of compilations on specific themes have been published in new U.S. editions since 1987 by Lotus Press, P.O. Box 325, Twin Lakes, WI 53181 U.S.A., www.lotuspress.com. Lotus Press also acts as a U.S. importer of books published by the Sri Aurobindo Ashram. Many university and college libraries are likely to have at least Sri Aurobindo's major works in their collections. The Library of Congress has more than 200 titles and editions by Sri Aurobindo. All questions regarding copyright and use of Sri Aurobindo's writings should be directed to the Copyright Department, Sri Aurobindo Ashram, Pondicherry, India 605002.

an introduction to the various aspects of his thought. Short of plunging into *The Life Divine* or *The Synthesis of Yoga*, both of which are essential for an understanding of Sri Aurobindo, the best source with which to begin is *Sri Aurobindo on Himself* and *The Mother, with Letters on the Mother*. These two books, containing letters with Sri Aurobindo's answers to the questions of his disciples, comprise his authoritative account of his early life, his years at Baroda, Calcutta, the years of spiritual realization, and the growing of the Ashram under the direction of the Mother. The standard brief account of the same topics is published in a popular sixty-page brochure, *Sri Aurobindo and His Ashram* (2001), which is almost entirely in Sri Aurobindo's own words.

Of the major works themselves, Sri Aurobindo's philosophical masterpiece *The Life Divine* can best be managed by beginning with the last six chapters. Another, and less orthodox way into *The Life Divine* would be to begin with the annotated Index (in the U.S. edition only), which runs for ninety pages and, like the Contents of Spinoza's *Ethics*, contains every proposition and hypothesis to be found in the text itself. Needless to say, the Index is only an outline at best; it is not substitute for the text itself, which is a philosophical, stylistic and organizational masterpiece. The best way into Sri Aurobindo's Integral Yoga is the fifty-page "Introduction" to *The Synthesis of Yoga*. The rest of this 1000-page work, which deals with "The Yoga of Divine Works," "The Yoga of Integral Knowledge," "The Yoga of Divine Love," and "The Yoga of Self-Perfection," is entirely lucid and intelligible. The three volumes titled "Letters on Yoga" Vol. 1, 2 and 3 contain Sri Aurobindo's letters, mostly to his disciples, on various aspects of his Yoga system. A large number of these letters have been organized thematically as an introduction to his teaching and the practice of the yoga in *The Integral Yoga: Sri Aurobindo's Teaching and Method of Practice*.

Secret of the Veda (On the Veda) is a scholarly interpretation of the Vedic hymns; the importance of this work is due to the prominent role of the Vedas in the development of Sri Aurobindo's vision. A companion volume *Hymns to the Mystic Fire* represents Sri Aurobindo's translation of all the hymns to Agni, the Divine flame, from the Rig Veda. Sri Aurobindo's translations of and extensive commentary on some of the major Upanishads, the great philosophical works of India, are set forth in *The Upanishads*. Even more prominent, and more immediately intelligible to most readers, is Sri Aurobindo's brilliant interpretation of the Bhagavad Gita, entitled *Essays on the Gita*. This work is an excellent introduction to Sri Aurobindo, to the *Gita*, and to the Indian religious and philosophical consciousness. Major portions of these essays have been integrated into the text and translation of the Bhagavad Gita in a work edited by Anilbaran Roy titled *Bhagavad Gita and Its Message*.

The Human Cycle: The Psychology of Social Development, The Ideal of Human Unity, and *War and Self-Determination*, have been published in one volume as a trilogy "depicting the historical process that the Time-Spirit employs in the elaboration of the divine plan in the evolution of human life." The first two of these works are also available separately as individual volumes. The theses of these works, especially of *The Human Cycle* (originally published in the *Arya* under the title *The Psychology of Social Development*), have survived more than eight decades with remarkable staying power; in all important respects they are as contemporary as the writings of William Ernest Hocking, F.S.C. Northrup, Karl Jaspers, or S. Radhakrishnan. Both *The Human Cycle: Psychology of Social Development* and *The Ideal of Human Unity* have recently been published as individual volumes in U.S. editions.

The Foundations of Indian Culture contains three essays in defense of Indian culture, and three essays specifically on Indian art, literature and poetry. This work not only serves as an excellent introduction to Sri Aurobindo and to Indian culture, it also reveals the extent to which Sri Aurobindo had absorbed and become a spokesman for the Indian cultural tradition.

Students of literature might begin with *Savitri: A Legend and a Symbol*, the epic poem which encompasses all of human life, history and aspirations within its wide-reaching scope, or with dramatic romance such as *Eric* or *Vasavadutta*, or with *The Future Poetry*, Sri Aurobindo's opinions on the history and future possibilities for English poetry. The extensive relationship between the practice of yoga and psychology has been explored at length in compilations from the writings of Sri Aurobindo and the Mother compiled by Dr. A.S. Dalal. These compilations explore issues of psychology thematically and include: *Living Within: The Yoga Approach to Psychological Health and Growth; The Hidden Forces of Life; Growing Within:*

The Psychology of Inner Development; Looking from Within: A Seeker's Guide to Attitudes for Mastery and Inner Growth; Powers Within; The Psychic Being: Soul -- Nature, Mission and Evolution; Our Many Selves: Practical Yogic Psychology, and Living Words: Soul-Kindlers for the New Millennium; Psychology, Mental Health and Yoga; A Greater Psychology: An Introduction to Sri Aurobindo's Thought.

Letters on Yoga contains Sri Aurobindo's correspondence with disciples in which he answers questions on his life, Yoga and vision. *Dictionary of Sri Aurobindo's Yoga,* compiled by M.P. Pandit, provides useful definitions and clarifications of the primary terminology found in Sri Aurobindo's writings.

A software CD ROM containing a large number of the main books of Sri Aurobindo has been published under the title *Sri Aurobindo Selected Writings Software CD ROM* version for Macintosh and Windows. This CD ROM includes search capabilities to search on key words across multiple volumes, as well as bookmarking and compilation capabilities.

WORKS BY SRI AUROBINDO'S DISCIPLES

The most distinguished of Sri Aurobindo's disciples was Sri Nolini Kanta Gupta, a close associate of Sri Aurobindo since their political activities in Bengal, and subsequently private secretary to Sri Aurobindo and the Mother. His collected works span eight volumes covering the entire range of Sri Aurobindo's life, political activities and yoga. M.P. Pandit, who wrote extensively on the Tantras and the Vedas, has also written several important works on Sri Aurobindo and the Mother. See especially *Sri Aurobindo and His Yoga.* (Twin Lakes, Wisconsin: Lotus Press, 1999). M.P. Pandit also wrote commentaries on *The Synthesis of Yoga* in a series including *The Yoga of Works, The Yoga of Love, The Yoga of Knowledge* and *The Yoga of Self Perfection.* For insight into the depths of *Savitri: A Legend and a Symbol,* see his 10 volume series titled *Readings in Savitri.* There are also several one-volume introductions to Sri Aurobindo's thought, the best of which are probably S.K. Maitra, *An Introduction to the Philosophy of Sri Aurobindo* (1965), Haridas Chaudhuri, *Sri Aurobindo: The Prophet of the Life Divine* (1951; 2nd rev. ed., 1960), K. R. Srinivas Iyengar, *Sri Aurobindo: A Biography and a History,* a massive two-volume work of comprehensive scope, and Georges van Vrekhem's *Beyond Man: The Life and Work of Sri Aurobindo and the Mother*. There are several biographies of Sri Aurobindo written by his disciples. The standard work is A.B. Purani's *Life of Sri Aurobindo*. M.P. Pandit has written a biography and life-sketch which appeared under the title *Sri Aurobindo* in the series Builders of Indian Philosophy. Keshavmurti has published *Sri Aurobindo: The Hope of Man* and Sisir Kumar Mitra, who made extensive use of Sri Aurobindo's private papers and records has written *Sri Aurobindo: Liberator*. Of more recent vintage is *Sri Aurobindo: A Brief Biography* written by Peter Heehs.

Other Studies on Sri Aurobindo

The most diverse single volume on Sri Aurobindo's thought is Haridas Chaudhuri and Frederic Spiegelberg (eds.), *The Integral Philosophy of Sri Aurobindo, A Commemorative Symposium* (London: George Allen and Unwin, 1960). This collection includes essays on Sri Aurobindo's philosophy, psychology, Yoga, and literature, by such scholars as S.K. Maitra, Charles A. Moore, Ernest Wood, Ninian Smart, Indra Sen, Pitirim Sorokin, Hajime Nakamura, and T.M.P. Mahadevan.

Among the studies of Sri Aurobindo's career prior to 1910, Jyotish Chandra Ghose's *Sri Aurobindo* (Calcutta: Samabaya Press, 1929, 1951 has the advantage of being written by a participant in Bengal politics; it also includes a sixty-eight-page transcript of Deshabandhu Das's defense of Sri Aurobindo in the famous Alipore bombing (a bomb thrown at the carriage of a District Magistrate had killed two women in it). For Sri Aurobindo's political activity and thought during his Calcutta years, see the Introduction to Haridas and Uma Mukherjee, *Sri Aurobindo and the New Thought in Indian Politics*, and a brief but excellent study by Karan Singh, *Prophet of Indian Nationalism: A Study of the Political Thought of Sri Aurobindo Ghose, 1983-1910* [London: George Allen and Unwin, 1963). The full course of Sri Aurobindo's political thought is treated in greater detail in V.P. Varma, *Political Philosophy of Sri Aurobindo* (New York: Asia Publishing House, 1960).

Among the more comprehensive studies of Sri Aurobindo's life and thought, the two most adequate are R.R. Diwakar, *Mahayogi Sri Aurobindo* (Bombay: Bharatiya Vidya Bhavan,

1967), and G.H. Langley, *Sri Aurobindo: India's Poet, Philosopher and Mystic* (London: David Marlowe Ltd., 1949). Nathaniel Pearson's *Sri Aurobindo and the Soul Quest of Man* (London: George Allen and Unwin, 1952) explicates the first 12 chapters of Sri Aurobindo's *The Life Divine*. Ram Shankar Misra, *The Integral Advaitism of Sri Aurobindo* (Banares: Banaras Hindu University, 1957), argues that Sri Aurobindo's metaphysical system is closer to classical Advaita Vedanta than is usually acknowledged. Finally, for an analysis and a criticism of integration and descent in Sri Aurobindo's theory of evolution, see Eliot Deutsch's "Sri Aurobindo's Interpretation of Spiritual Experience: A Critique," *International Philosophical Quarterly*, IV, 4 (December 1964).

YOGA AND INTEGRAL PHILOSOPHY

There are many editions of Patanjali's *Yoga Sutras*, the most authoritative being *The Yoga System of Patanjali*, with commentary of Vyasa and glossary of Vacaspati Misra, translated by J.H. Woods ("Oriental Series," XVII, Cambridge, Mass.: Harvard University Press, 1927). Among the more popular editions see *Raja Yoga* by Swami Vivekananda (Calcutta: Advaita Ashrama, 1976), A. Bahm, *Yoga: Union with the Ultimate* (New York: Frederick Ungar Publishing Company, 1964), Prabhavananda and Isherwood, *How to Know God: The Yoga Aphorisms of Patanjali* (Hollywood, California: Vedanta Press).Ernest Wood and Mircea Eliade have each written scholarly and popular works on Yoga philosophy and techniques. In general, Eliade emphasizes the religious and phenomenological aspects of Yoga and Wood emphasizes the Raja Yoga system, especially as developed by Patanjali and Sankara. Eliade's *Yoga: Freedom and Immortality* (New York: Pantheon Books, 1958) presents Yoga as the key to Indian consciousness; his more popular work *Patanjali and Yoga*, translated by Charles Lam Markham (New York: Fund and Wagnalls, 1969), offers a highly readable account of Patanjali's Yoga and the techniques of Yoga in various traditions. Ernest Wood's great work is *Practical Yoga: Ancient and Modern* (New York: E.P. Dutton, 1948); his less technical works are *Yoga* (Baltimore: Penguin Books, 1959), probably the most readable and scholarly paperback volume treating Patanjali's Yoga system, and *Great Systems of Yoga* (New York: Philosophical

Library, 1954), which is probably the best elementary survey of the various schools of Hatha and Raja Yoga. Alain Danielou, *Yoga: The Method of Re-Integration* (New York: University Books, 1955) is an excellent study of the principles and practices of Hatha, Raja, and other forms of Yoga.

For a more philosophical account of the Samkya-Yoga system of Patanjali, see S. Dasgupta, *Yoga as Philosophy and Religion* (New York: E.P. Dutton, 1924) and *Yoga Philosophy in Relation to Other Systems of Indian Philosophy I* (Cambridge: Cambridge University Press, 1922), and Gerald James Larson, *Classical Samkya: An Interpretation of Its History and Meaning* (Delhi: Motilal Banarsidass, 1969). There are also many publications available from the more prominent contemporary schools of Yoga: the Ramakrishna-Vivekananda Centers, which are in many cities in America and abroad, stock the writings of Sri Ramakrishna (see especially *The Gospel of Sri Ramakrishna*) and Swami Vivekananda (see especially the *Collected Works*, 8 vols., and *Selections from Swami Vivekananda*). Similarly, the works of Swami Sivananda and his disciples are available from Sivananda Ashram, Rishikesh, India; see especially Rammurti S. Misra, *Textbook of Yoga Psychology* (New York: The Julian Press, 1963).

For an informed survey of the great living Yogis and the major Yoga centers of India, see Alfonso Caycedo, *The India of Yogis* (New Delhi: National Publishing House, 1966).

Westerners interested in Yoga cannot afford to ignore Carl Jung's warning concerning the application of Yoga to the peoples of the West; see "Yoga and the West", *Psychology and Religion: West and East*, translated by R.F.C. Hull ("Bollingen Series," XX, New York: Pantheon Books, 1958), pp. 529-538.

For helpful accounts of Sri Aurobindo in relation to contemporary Indian thinkers such as Ramakrishna, Vivekananda, Tagore, Gandhi, Radhakrishnan, Bhattacharya, and Iqbal, see R.S. Srivastava, *Contemporary Indian Philosophy* (Delhi: Munshiram Manoharlal, 1967), and V.S. Naravane, *Modern Indian Thought* (New York: Asia Publishing House, 1964).

Despite their very different theories of Yoga, Maya, Brahman, and history, Radhakrishnan and Sri Aurobindo are frequently compared as philosophers of an East-West synthesis, spiritual experience, and evolution. It is interesting to compare Radhakrishnan's *An Idealist View of Life* (London: George Allen and Unwin, 1929) with Sri Aurobindo's *The Life*

Divine, Radhakrishnan's *Bhagavadgita* (London: George Allen and Unwin, 1953) with Sri Aurobindo's *Essays on the Gita*, and Radhakrishnan's *Kalki—or the Future of Civilization* (Bombay: Hind Kitabs, 1926, 1956) or *Religion in a Changing World* (New York: Humanities Press, 1967) with Sri Aurobindo's *The Human Cycle* or *The Ideal of Human Unity*. For a paperback collection of Radhakrishnan's writings, see my *Radhakrishnan: Selected Writings on Philosophy, Religion and Culture* (New York: E.P. Dutton, 1970).

Although there are no Western thinkers who have a grasp of Yoga comparable to Sri Aurobindo's, Henri Bergson's *Creative Evolution* (New York: Modern Library, 1935, 1953) and more recently Pierre Teilhard de Chardin's *Phenomenon of Man* (New York: Harper and Row, 1959) and *The Future of Man* (New York: Harper and Row, 1964) beg comparison with Sri Aurobindo's theories of human evolution. The American philosophical tradition, including Charles Peirce, Josiah Royce, William James, and John Dewey, has consistently emphasized human and natural evolution; this tradition may be said to culminate in Alfred North Whitehead's *Process and Reality* (New York: Macmillan Company, 1929). Haridas Chaudhuri's *The Philosophy of Integralism* (1967) combines Western insights with a metaphysical framework provided by Sri Aurobindo. His *Integral Yoga: The Concept of Harmonious and Creative Living* (London, 1965, reprinted 1970) makes a survey of the traditional Yoga systems of India culminating in a comprehensive synthesis of the spiritual aspirations of East and West. V. Madhusudan Reddy's *Sri Aurobindo's Philosophy of Evolution* (Hyderabad: Institute of Human Study, 1966), abounds in comparisons between Sri Aurobindo and Western philosophers such as Royce, Bergson, and Whitehead. Similarly S.K. Maitra's *The Meeting of East and West in Sri Aurobindo's Philosophy* (1968) compares Sri Aurobindo with Plato, Plotinus, Hartmann, Hegel, Bergson and Whitehead.

NOTES ON THE TEXT

Sri Aurobindo's contribution to his Ashram's *Bulletin of Physical Education* (now the *Bulletin of the Sri Aurobindo International Centre of Education*) during 1949-1950, were first published by the Sri Aurobindo Ashram Press in 1952 under the title, *The Supramental Manifestation Upon Earth,* and were published as *The Mind of Light* by E.P. Dutton in 1953. The book was reissued by Dutton in paperback format in 1971 with the kind permission of the Mother of the Sri Aurobindo Ashram, Pondicherry India. This current printing is the first Lotus Press edition in 2003, and includes an added introductory outline written by Sri Aurobindo describing "The Teaching of Sri Aurobindo," along with an updated, revised and enlarged bibliography.

Although the present title does not sufficiently emphasize the levels of consciousness above the mental, it has been retained because it is well established in American bibliographies.

OTHER TITLES BY SRI AUROBINDO

Available from your local bookseller or
LOTUS PRESS, P.O. Box 325, Twin Lakes, WI 53181 USA
262/889-8561 • www.lotuspress.com
email: lotuspress@lotuspress.com

Sri Aurobindo
Rebirth and Karma

REBIRTH AND KARMA by Sri Aurobindo
In-depth study of the concepts of rebirth, karma and the higher lines of karma. One of the best introductions to this area we have ever found.
LOTUS PRESS   ISBN 0-941524-63-9   190 pp pb $9.95

THE LIFE DIVINE by Sri Aurobindo
The Life Divine is Sri Aurobindo's major philosophical exposition, spanning more than a thousand pages and integrating the major spiritual directions of mankind into a coherent picture of the growth of the spiritual essence of man through diverse methods, philosophies and spiritual practices.

LOTUS PRESS   ISBN 0-941524-62-0   1113 pp hb $39.95
LOTUS PRESS   ISBN 0-941524-61-2   1113 pp pb $29.95

Sri Aurobindo
The Life Divine

THE INTEGRAL YOGA
Sri Aurobindo's Teaching and Method of Practice
by Sri Aurobindo (compilation)

Sri Aurobindo
The Integral Yoga

"These carefully selected excerpts from the writings of Sri Aurobindo provide a wonderfully accessible entre into the writings of one of the great masters of spiritual synthesis."
Ram Dass
LOTUS PRESS   ISBN 0-941524-76-0   416 pp pb $14.95

SYNTHESIS OF YOGA, US EDITION by Sri Aurobindo
In *The Synthesis of Yoga* Sri Aurobindo unfolds his vision of an integral yoga embracing all the powers and activities of man. First, he reviews the three great yogic paths of Knowledge, Works and Love, along with Hatha Yoga, Raja Yoga and Tantra, and then integrates them all into a great symphony. "Truth of philosophy is of a merely theoretical value unless it can be lived, and we have therefore tried in the *The Synthesis of Yoga* to arrive at a synthetical view of the principles and methods of the various lines of spiritual self-discipline and the way in which they can lead to an integral divine life in the human existence".

Sri Aurobindo
The Synthesis of Yoga

LOTUS PRESS   ISBN 0-941524-66-3   899 pp hb $34.95
LOTUS PRESS   ISBN 0-941524-65-5   889 pp pb $29.95

Available from your local bookseller or
Lotus Press, PO Box 325, Twin Lakes, WI 53181 • 262-889-8561
www.lotuspress.com • email: lotuspress@lotuspress.com